Secrets in the Family

Secrets in the Family

Transforming the Shame and Hurt
into Openness and Love

CONTEMPORARY
BOOKS

CHICAGO · NEW YORK

Library of Congress Cataloging-in-Publication Data

Mumey, Jack.
  Secrets in the family.

  1. Family—Mental health.   2. Shame.   3. Family
psychotherapy.   I. Title.
RC488.5.M86   1989   158'.24   89-15833
ISBN 0-8092-4410-1

Published by Contemporary Books, Inc.
180 North Michigan Avenue, Chicago, Illinois 60601
Manufactured in the United States of America
International Standard Book Number: 0-8092-4410-1

Published simultaneously in Canada by Beaverbooks, Ltd.
195 Allstate Parkway, Valleywood Business Park
Markham, Ontario L3R 4T8 Canada

For Cyn
with love and affection

Contents

Acknowledgments

This project was born from my personal conviction that families continue to stay in a trap of their own making, a trap that can be sprung only if the family members are willing to take certain risks of disclosure about themselves and about the things they have been hiding.

So many people have contributed to my idea bank over the years as a therapist that it would be impossible to acknowledge them all. Suffice it to say that every patient and every family with whom I am privileged to work adds a dimension to my own understanding of how human beings develop elaborate ways to hurt—and not nearly enough ways to heal. I am grateful to all of them for casting a light into the shadows, helping me to see.

My beautiful wife, Cynthia, has been a great inspiration to me, believing that all things are possible. My four children, Jackson, Tracey, Dana, and Dawn, are not only proud boosters of their dad's efforts, but severe critics and watchdogs of his failings, a good balance for both a father and an author!

My partner, Paul Staley, provides such daily inspiration for how things should be done that not enough credit could ever go to him. My editor, Shari Lesser Wenk, has not only the patience and the skill of an editor, but the virtue of being able to guide my efforts so that they become the best of what I can achieve; she will settle for nothing less! Editor Jodi Block has been with this project from the beginning, and her guidance has been valuable indeed.

Thank you, all!

Secrets in the Family

1
The Elephant in the Living Room

Well, here you are back home for a visit, the first time in months. The family sits at breakfast, and *nobody* is going to say one word about what happened last night! What's the matter with everyone? *You* heard Dad and Mom in another heated replay of World War II. *You* know this was mainly caused because they were both drinking again, heavily.

And now, here everyone sits, acting perfectly normal, talking, but not *really* talking. What you want to know is why nobody has the guts to talk about the damn drinking that leads to these monumental battles!

To your right is your younger brother; *he* must have heard! And across from you is Grandma ... how could she possibly *not* have heard? And what's worse, you are all adults! Then it strikes you right square between the scrambled eggs and bacon on your plate: There's another guest in your home! This guest has been around ever since *you* have! It's an elephant in your living room!

Yes, an elephant! It's been standing there in front of everybody, and they all see that elephant, but nobody talks about it.

1

Thus, you are trapped in a "family secret." In this case, it's the alcohol abuse that goes on every weekend. Here you have come back to see the family, full of expectations that things are different, and nothing's changed! Everyone is still protecting the family secret that Mom and Dad drink alcoholically and have for years. Everyone sits there at the table making small talk and acting as if *absolutely nothing happened last night.*

You suddenly feel a terrible rush of anger. It starts way down in your toes and begins to surge up through your whole body until it's stuck right at your throat. Unable to control it any longer, you toss a half-eaten piece of toast onto your plate and explode, "What the hell's the *matter* with all of you?"

"What's eating *you?*" your mother replies, in her sophisticated, very controlled way.

"Bacon and eggs not good enough for our big-city gal?" your father laughs as he gulps some more black coffee. Even Grandma now comes to life with, "Really, Jennifer! Do we need such outbursts at breakfast? And your first day home, too."

You feel the tears welling up in your eyes; you push, or rather shove, yourself away from the table and run back to your room, reminiscent of the way you stuffed anger and other feelings when you were a little girl. As you round the landing, you can hear them say, "Whatever in the world is the matter with *her?*"

But you know the answer; you finally realized that elephant in your living room has been there all along and that it took getting away from your family long enough to finally see how large an elephant it is and how long your family has looked at it but never, ever talked about it.

Well, you are definitely not alone. Millions of families have the same things going on in their lives, family secrets that work not to heal but to *hurt.* That's what this book is all about: helping you get some tools for uncovering and dealing with the family secrets that have kept you in emotional chains for years. You may spend days, weeks, months, and years working on your *physical* attitudes but have allowed these old family secrets to eat away at your emotional self, keeping you in a hurting mode, a mode that needs to be turned into healing, so that you can truly enjoy all the fruits of life.

The worst part of all of this is that *you* have been a very big part of keeping that family elephant right where it is, in the middle of your living room. If everyone sees it but no one talks about it, it just stays there, sometimes longer than any of the living family members!

What you will learn from reading this book is something about family secrets and the ways you can turn this hurting into healing, the ways you can get rid of this elephant and never have to worry about it taking up so much space in your lives again!

This little scenario used alcohol abuse as the "family secret," but you are certainly aware that there are dozens of events that can be classified as secrets. So, let's come up with a definition of just what *is* a family secret.

Basically, a family secret is any event, past or present, that is known by all the principals of the family but never discussed outside the family circle. That definition covers family secrets as viewed by the *outside* world, but what about those secrets like the one in the scenario where the secret isn't even talked about inside the family? So let's add to our definition, thus: A family secret is any event, past or present, whose disclosure inside or outside the family circle threatens the safety of the family and therefore remains locked within the confines of individual family members.

Safety is a key word in this definition, because that's really the fodder for that big old elephant. The family has always placed safety as the premium to survival, banding together from the earliest cave clans to the present. Keeping a family secret means that no one inside or outside the family "clan" can have a "weapon" (knowledge of the secret) to destroy the family. Makes sense, doesn't it?

It also makes sense that you have been programmed into

being a participant in this age-old process of never hanging out the dirty laundry, and are probably perpetuating the practice in your own life now. It doesn't matter if you are not yet a married or cohabiting person with a family of your own; you can be single, on your own, and still feeding that old elephant by *keeping* secrets that maintain you in a hurting position instead of a healthy one.

There are many classifications of secrets, but let's look at a choice few categories of human behavior (or misbehavior) that we can easily denote as family secrets. Only you, of course, know *your* family secret(s), but maybe one of these really hits home for you:

- Alcoholism or drug abuse
- Adoption
- Divorce
- Incest
- Rape
- White-collar crime
- Battering
- Imprisonment
- Adultery
- Bankruptcy
- Abortion
- Disease
- Homosexuality
- Learning disability
- Bigotry
- Forced marriage
- Secret lives of fantasy
- Poverty
- Illegitimacy
- Active crime life

These possibilities are just for openers. You may have looked at this list and found at least one of these items in your family "closet," but you may also have found that your family secret isn't on the list at all. If that's the case, then you might ask, "Since my family secret isn't of major proportions such as those on the list, it can't be very harmful, right?"

Wrong! Just because your family secret doesn't conveniently fit the ones listed in no way takes away from the magnitude of the harm a family secret can do! The criterion is whether the *keeping* of this secret has in any manner whatsoever prevented growth, either yours or that of some other loved family member.

In our scenario at the beginning of this chapter, the alcohol abuse of the mother and father is in itself a problem. The fact that the family refuses to acknowledge and discuss the drinking has contributed to the terrible guilt, frustration, and anger that either or both of the adult children may have been experiencing about their own irrational behavior in life.

If they had been able to openly identify themselves as adult children of alcoholics at an earlier stage, the children might have had a better chance to stop the hurting and get on with the healing. The family secret, however, got in the way and *stayed* in the way.

This book isn't just about alcoholism; it's about *whatever* secret has been preserved and even nurtured down through the ages, to your distinct harm! At this point you have a right to ask just how that secret is hurting you. You might even have said to yourself, "I don't give a damn what they do or did . . . I only need to take care of me!"

The problem with that kind of thinking is that the secret *does* affect you and how you behave. If you consider that your "life script" is written when you are four or five years old, then you must know that your behavior through life is going to be influenced by all the elements of family life that you have experienced. By "life script" I mean the way in which you will probably function on a social, physical, and emotional basis with regard to life's situations and problems.

For example, consider a family where it's been viewed as OK ever since you can remember for family members to refer to blacks as "niggers." That term is abhorrent to you, as it well should be, and yet for years and years, you and the rest of the family heard that offensive term used over and over by your grandfather and your father. It has affected you to this day. You may wonder why you have a difficult time working with or being friendly with the blacks in your office; you may experience a flashback to the degrading manner in which blacks were always addressed in your family, the ways in which those family members were allowed to continue this bigotry without challenge; and now you are feeling a conflict of emotions.

This conflict is understandable, but inexcusable. I have a patient who has decided that he is no longer going to participate in racially oriented "jokes." It's a part of his personal wellness program to stop the chain of that kind of thing, beginning with himself. To this day, Mel will stop you when you say, "I've got a joke for you!"

"Is this an ethnic joke?" he will ask, and before you can reply, he will say, "Because if it is, I don't want to hear it!"

You may think his behavior is pretty stodgy or old-fashioned or narrow in its own right. But during the course of our therapy together, Mel realized that racial bigotry had been a great part of his early childhood, and through therapy he realized that he needed to confront the people in his life who perpetuated such bigotry.

Mel had once had a torrid love affair with a black woman: educated, beautiful, and a talented musician, as was he, but the affair unleashed a family secret. He was considering making this woman his life companion, until his family got wind of it. Their response was to spout off a string of epithets against "niggers" and other equally degrading words of description, which made Mel cringe. He never realized that relations with black people were such a vehement family issue; they all were living in modern times, in the eighties, when discrimination is supposed to be a thing of the past.

The more Mel took this abuse over his relationship, the more he sensed there was something else to his family's unbridled venom aimed at blacks. He continued to confront the issue until his grandfather blurted out the family secret.

"Your no-good uncle tried to pull that crap on us!" Grandfather shouted at Mel. "Wanting to bring his nigger wife into *our* family!"

Mel was totally blown away by this piece of news. His father's brother, long since dead, was never mentioned in the family. There were no family pictures of him anywhere, and only through "slips" now and then as Mel was growing up did he even realize that he had an uncle. The family had "buried" the uncle and his secret deep, deep into a metaphorical closet. Mel's own love affair forced the door of that closet open and caused shock waves from which it took Mel a long time to recover.

The family secret kept Mel from following the course of his life with the lovely black woman with whom he was involved. He could not go against the family, and so he miserably dumped his lady friend and became increasingly melancholy.

When Mel's family got wind of the demise of the relationship, everything was peaches and cream again. Mel, who had not been welcome for Sunday dinner, was suddenly at the top of the list. But when Mel tried to discuss his uncle's marriage to a black woman, the family clammed up. It was not a topic for discussion again, and the whole episode was put down to the uncle being a ne'er-do-well gambler and whoremonger who had come to a miserable end because of his own evil ways—not the least of those "evils" being his marriage outside his own race.

Mel tried over and over to get his family to talk about this chapter in their lives, all to no avail. As a result, whenever he heard racially oriented jokes or stories, Mel was filled with a rage he could not explain. It was as if the whole burden of his family's terrible bigotry and cover-up about a family member had come to roost with Mel.

So Mel fought back in his own small but important way along the path to healing. He decided that at least *he* would not foster the continuation of bigotry through humor. It cost him some friends who thought he had become high and mighty, "too good" for the rest of them, and he endured the usual taunts of "goody two-shoes" and other such name-calling.

But Mel stuck to his guns, and as we continued to work together in therapy, I could see him having some small but important impact on others around him at our Gateway Treatment Center. They began to learn that Mel, who was a very good joke teller, was no longer going to be interested in hearing racially oriented jokes, so they stopped telling them.

Mel has distanced himself from his family; he has written to them to say he is unhappy with their continuing to foster their bigotry and with their obvious unwillingness to get their family secret about his Uncle Fred out in the open and deal with it.

The response from Mel's family has been predictable; the problem is all his. "Obviously," wrote his mother in a letter he shared with me, "instead of helping you, your therapy is just driving a wedge between us!" For Mel, these have been both hurtful and helpful times. He continues to hurt about the family and the secret they continue to harbor, which alienates him from them. His lost romance has become even more of a bitter pill for him to swallow because he realizes that he caved in to his family's pressures to stop seeing this woman.

The healing part for him is his continued one-man battle against ethnic humor and his realization that he must continue to try to get his family to acknowledge the elephant that runs amok in their living room even today. Mel believes his persistence will pay off, that he will prevail with his family, and his determination is part of his entire recovery program.

Family secrets are like weeds in your garden of life. If you continue to let them grow, they will take over the garden, and you will get less and less of the fruits and vegetables that you were planning to enjoy. But there is hope! As you progress through this book, you can learn to recognize and dig out those weeds. Remember that your primary mission is not to be able to go into the midst of your family circle like "Crusader Rabbit," but rather to start the talking process that will help you more clearly understand what is making *you* tick!

We all need the opportunity to practice wellness, but if we don't pick up the hoe and do a little of the hard work, the weeds will win the battle of the garden. If you go back to basics, you can rely on the fact that for every action there is an equal reaction.

You behave in your life today as the result of the input from many sources, your "life script," if you will. The process you will learn in this book is a little bit of editing of that script! You will explore ways in which changes can be made in your life. This prospect may seem both exciting and scary, but you can handle it.

Making a change is always a little scary; we become comfortable with the way things are. We play "old tapes" because we understand those tapes and they don't frighten us. New tapes that play songs of change to us can be scary because they will be leading us into taking action that involves risk.

But go ahead and plunge right into the deep water of your family secrets. By so doing, maybe you can take responsibility for yourself. Now that's exciting! The growth you can achieve from taking that risk can be very worthwhile.

2
Facing Anxieties

One of my favorite comic strips is Berke Breathed's creation, "Bloom County." If you follow this strip, you are aware of one of the characters named Binkley, and of his closet of anxieties. Every so often, particularly on a Sunday morning, you will open your paper and find Binkley staring at an incredible monster in his closet. It is classic humor that points out the closet of anxieties that all humans have.

But how does this little cartoon character deal with and face his anxieties? He *talks* about them; he shares them with someone else. For a listener, Binkley picks his father; Binkley climbs up on his chest and unleashes whatever anxiety is pressing his young mind to the limits.

The burden of carrying around these deep and troubled thoughts can be too much for anyone, and you don't have to tolerate that for yourself. A fair start would be for you to admit that something is going on with you that you don't quite understand. Talking with someone can and will unleash what that "something" is; the process may be frightening, opening up that closet of anxiety, but it is absolutely necessary.

Imagine you are deep in thought; say you're shopping downtown, looking for that special gift, and have been going from store to store, not quite finding anything that suits you.

"Well," you think, "maybe across the street, in that little boutique over there, I will find the wedding gift I need!"

Without really thinking, you step off the curb and into the path of traffic. Suddenly a horn honks; you look and instantly jump back up on the curb. Your heart begins to pound with the surge of adrenaline that has entered your system; you feel weak in the knees and maybe a little faint because of the close call. You didn't stop and *think* about whether you should jump back on the curb; rather it was an instant, involuntary set of actions and reactions that went into play to save your life.

Now comes the anxiety. Supposing you never told anyone about this incident. Let's say you just stuff it in your closet and forget about it until one day you have to be downtown, and you start to cross a street and maybe, just maybe, you *can't* do it! You don't even get off the sidewalk. You feel paralyzed with fear; sweat begins to pour from you; and you really feel as if you are going to faint.

What's happened? Has the street become any different from any other street that combines traffic and pedestrians? Of course not. What's happened is that you have become immobilized and unable to act because of the fear that has been locked inside you. You opened a door one time and found a bear standing there; frightened, you slammed the door. Now you're afraid to open *any* door, convinced there will be a bear standing there. Funny how the mind works, creating an anxiety, an unreasoning fear about crossing streets. So what you need to do is open that closet and let out the anxiety.

You do this by talking. You tell someone—friend, relative, or co-worker perhaps—about the incident of nearly getting hit while crossing the street. The more you tell it, the more the anxiety will disappear. The more you stuff the incident, the larger it will loom in the dark recesses of your mind until one day

it will burst forth like one of Binkley's green-and-purple monsters.

So for you, hurting with the burden of some family secret, you
are well advised to share that anxiety. That doesn't mean you
take it upon yourself to give away the family secret. You'll travel
down *that* path a little later on in this book. For now, let's just
concentrate on recognizing and dealing with anxiety.

If you have been feeling on edge and out of sorts, if you are
nervous, tense, and irritable, then maybe you are the victim of at
least one anxiety. The longer you continue to stuff these anxieties, the harder they are to deal with. The best way, for example,
that I work with people who are afraid to fly, is to tell them, "Talk
about it! Describe your fear to the person sitting next to you on
the plane."

The reason for this is that, as soon as you give voice to your
anxiety, it begins to dissipate like a cloud of smoke. It's the
stuffing of your feelings that makes you act nervous or tense.
When you read those symptoms, you become aware that you
have even given yourself physical discomfort by keeping your
anxieties tightly locked in your "closet." They need to be let out,
and that's really what therapy is all about. You are able, through
therapy, to disclose your fears or anxieties and work through the
solutions to them.

When you have a chance to disclose the things that are locked
inside, you are helping share the burden with someone else. But
be careful; this doesn't mean you also share the responsibility.
You are totally responsible for your feelings; therapy simply gives
you the opportunity to safely disclose them. A therapist will help
you see other ways that you can deal with the anxieties, methods
to solve your problems and not make them the reasons for
inaction on your part.

Many times I will tell our patients, "To get really well, you
have to be sick and tired of *being* sick and tired!" When you let
anxiety control your life, then you remain in a state of constant
anxiety. So what to do? Maybe you don't have or can't afford a

private therapist. Fair enough, but what about your local mental health association? You may have to be on a waiting list, but people *are* there who can help you. Everything you say is treated in confidentiality, so you don't have to fear disclosure. You can even share with a priest, rabbi, or minister, either formally through the confessional process or through meetings on an individual basis. Your secret will remain safe. This gives you a way to get over the anxieties that are associated with that secret.

Although you may not be ready to reveal the family secret, what's important is for you to understand that keeping the family secret deep inside you is causing you to feel anxious and afraid of something, of living your life, of making decisions and moving ahead!

The first step is to acknowledge that you have an anxiety. If you are working with a therapist, he or she will help you unlock the relationship of your anxiety to your family secret. At this point, it might be fine for you just to accept that the two are related, even though the connection may seem remote.

This is certainly not to suggest that every anxiety or fear is caused by the family secret. Simply be aware that if you have been stuffing your fears and anxieties the way you have stuffed the family secret, then they are related. You are not talking about or dealing with either one, and so the anxieties grow and grow.

You don't have the right to disclose the family secret at this point, although Chapter 4 will look at who needs to "own" the family secret; it may or may not be you. For now, that isn't important. Simply acknowledge that some of your anxieties may arise because you are burdening yourself with carrying around this excess baggage.

You may not even be aware that there *is* a connection between the anxieties that you feel and the family secret. Let's take a simple example.

Suppose you are a man who is contemplating marriage. You are putting off making the commitment because every time you think about it, you get cold feet and all the other classic symptoms associated with this kind of stage fright. So, you decide (probably under pressure from the special lady involved) to look at your problem.

Let's say that your family secret involves male members never being able to stay in a marriage for very long. Or let's take it a step further and say that none of the men in your family, including your father, have *ever* stayed married. This can create quite an anxiety for you, particularly if you are dedicated to the idea that marriage can and should be a one-time experience.

You may actually believe that you've inherited some sort of genetic flaw that affects the men in your family. It may sound silly, but it isn't. I treated a patient who had that very fear. Locked deep inside him was the belief that he could not and would not stay married. He had never shared the secret, and it took quite a lot of therapy to get to what the real problem was. What *was* the real family secret?

His mother and father had been married for some years when the father left home. His mother waited for his father to get his head together and come home to her, but he stayed away for two years. In the meantime, this young man's mother divorced his father and married "on the rebound" a man she thought she loved. It wasn't to be either, and they were divorced.

Then the first husband turned up on the scene again and began to court his wife all over. He moved back into the household, and before you knew it, a son was born. The young man we've been talking about was their son. There was just one problem: Mom and Dad failed to get remarried. This young man, then, technically was illegitimate.

The family had kidded about all this for years: Mom and Dad had always shrugged it off and said, "What difference does it make? We were married before and didn't ever change the *important* papers or anything!" When the mother had remarried, she had kept her first married name; therefore, in *her* eyes, she was still technically "Mrs. Barker" (a fictional name, like all those used in this book).

No wonder the young man was afraid to make a commitment and was carrying around a whole bunch of anxiety about marriage. *His* only life experience was based on a deep and, for him, dark family secret involving marriage, divorce, and remating without the benefit of a legal marriage.

It took quite a while to get to the base of this "marriage anxiety," but we finally did it. Once the family secret bounced out of this man's closet, his anxiety could be identified, worked on, and *finally* dissipated. As this book is being written, he and the woman he loves have gotten so far as to make a formal engagement. Marriage, I think, is not too far away.

Some questions you might want to ask to help with your own "anxiety closet" are:

- "What's making me feel the way I do?"
- "Am I tired of feeling this way?"
- "What's making me not take any action to change?"
- "How can I get started?"
- "What do I need to do to label (talk about) this?"
- "With whom can I share this anxiety?"
- "Where do I go to share it (friend, church, group)?"
- "When do I get started?"
- "Am I ready to give up this anxiety?"
- "Am I using this anxiety to stay sick?"

"Sick," as used in this last question, means staying in the same place in the situation where you find yourself. That is, you are "sick" if you are not making the changes that will enhance your life, but are comfortable with the way you are behaving.

The anxiety is controlling you instead of you controlling and conquering it. That's *not* going to be acceptable if you are to overcome these anxieties. You must be willing *not* to stay in a state of "sickness" but to haul those anxieties out of your closet and face them head-on. They are far less frightening in the harsh reality of daylight than in the dark and mysterious closet where you have kept them.

Do you remember going through "spook houses" on Halloween when you were a kid? Or maybe you have even *been* one of
the featured attractions at one of these places, which are so
popular as a means of providing safe and sane Halloween fun.

When all the lights are on in the spook house, it isn't spooky
at all. Quite the contrary; it lacks almost all of the punch that
you are trying to provide. But as soon as the lights are extin-
guished and the special effects are added—different lighting,
sounds—the "spooks" can be really scary.

It's the same way with your anxieties. As long as you keep
them in the dark, all spooky and wrapped in deep mystery, they
will appear to be larger and more deadly than they really are;
they will appear to be more in control of your life than they
really are. They will seem to be unsolvable as problems in your
life. Even more frightening, they will keep you from moving into
a state of wellness, and you will remain locked in a world where
anxiety is so much a part of your life that you never spend a day
without it. That's a horrible feeling, and exactly what we're
working to overcome. Take a clue from Binkley and drag those
monsters out of your "anxiety closet."

Of course, not all anxieties are related to family secrets. Nor is
everything that's wrong with you or me caused by family issues.
But look at the *possibility* that some of the anxieties that you are
keeping locked up in your closet are rooted in family secrets. By
asking the questions listed earlier, you will identify those anxieties that are based on family secrets and those that are not.
Either way, of course, the healthy thing to do is drag them out of
the closet and deal with them. Letting the light of day strike
them is like letting the sun's first rays strike the mythical vampire
and driving him back to his coffin forever.

You have been haunted long enough! The rest of this book
will help you find the ways to get back on the right track. You will
do this in the coming chapters through the following steps:

 1. Identifying the problem (What's going on around here,
    anyway?)

2. Fixing the responsibility (Who needs to *own* the secret?)
3. Assessing the impact on friends, neighbors, and co-workers
4. Offering solutions to yourself
5. Handling objections and put-offs to the solutions
6. Closing the deal, that is, getting started on the solutions
7. Monitoring results (How's my life changing?)
8. Watching out for failure
9. Identifying and handling family "saboteurs"
10. Realizing the payoffs for getting well
11. Erasing the stigma of family secrets
12. Learning what you can do for "preventive maintenance"
13. Recognizing how you can and *will* enjoy the healing!

Want to come along on this track? Want to take a few risks and open up that closet of anxieties? Of course! Family secrets have been keeping you down long enough; they've been keeping the *family* down long enough.

3

Identifying the Problem

What's going on around your household? Is every member of your family jumping down the throat of every other member? Has the usual family harmony seemed to have turned into a screeching match between any two or three people gathered together in the same room?

This description is probably making you feel a little queasy, reminding you that that's exactly what seems to be happening around your house. And to complicate things, have you been in some kind of fog trying to find an answer to what's happening?

When family members become dysfunctional, then it isn't long until the family, as a unit, becomes equally dysfunctional. And you keep trying to put the pieces back together, trying in vain to excuse the behavior that every family member is displaying or "acting out" at the moment.

So, you rightfully go to your old standby bag of tapes and play them, seeking some solution to the problem. Maybe your tapes contain one of the following messages:

- "The summer heat is getting to everyone."

- "Jerry is working much too hard; he needs to relax."
- "If these kids don't get a job soon, we'll all go nuts."
- "Why can't everyone just get along?"

These are just a few examples from almost everyone's bag of old tapes. You've probably got copies of them, plus your own unique messages in your old bag. But let's look at a new tape, and see if this one could sound different: "Maybe my family is acting this way because of what has happened to us."

The word *what* in this message refers to your family secret. Maybe you know the secret, and maybe other family members do and are simply stuffing it and being afraid to talk about it. Let me give you an example.

I was recently working with Matt, a man who had paid a visit back home for the first time in close to a year. He had been keeping in touch quite regularly with his mother and his grandmother. Both women lived together, so Matt would make a long Sunday phone call to them at least every other week.

When he went home, there were no elaborate plans for a special get-together or anything like that. Mom simply wanted to gather the clan and have a usual Saturday night dinner at her house. She had invited her married daughter and son-in-law, her brother and sister-in-law, and my patient's younger brother. So far, so good.

At the gathering, it was Grandmother who started pouring the drinks for everyone, and she poured with a vengeance. It was like déjà vu for Matt as he remembered how Saturday nights had been when he was growing up in this home. The only missing ingredient was his father, who had been divorced by his mother some years before. Matt was still in recovery from his own abuse of alcohol, so he did not drink any liquor but stayed with soft drinks.

Well, dinner got later and later, and almost all the other family members, led by Grandma and Mom, got pretty well oiled. Matt tolerated what was happening to a point and then finally took over the cooking of the steaks on the outdoor grill and became the party's host instead of "honored guest."

Here's what happened the next morning: absolutely nothing! That's right, *nothing*. The family gathered around the breakfast table and acted as if *nothing* had gotten out of hand. No one mentioned the loud arguments that had occurred between Mom and her mother (Grandma) or the bitter accusations that were flung back and forth between Matt's younger brother and his married sister.

Matt reported to me, "I just couldn't believe it! They all sat there around the breakfast table saying stuff like, 'More orange juice, honey?' and 'Please pass the toast,' but *no one* talked about how blitzed they had all been last night!"

"How did you feel sitting there and experiencing that?" I asked.

"I was *royally* pissed!" Matt exploded. "Why the hell wouldn't anyone talk about how out-of-hand things had gotten last night? It's as if absolutely nothing had happened!"

I asked Matt what had happened after breakfast, and he told me that the relatives began making a lot of little backbiting remarks to one another.

"Oh, they started off being kind of funny, and I thought it would stop soon. But it didn't. In fact, it got worse—so bad that my sister got up from her chair in tears and ran up to her room, just the way she used to do when we were kids. Hell, this is my married sister, and she was acting like she was thirteen years old!"

So, here sat Matt, a couple of thousand miles away from his own home, witnessing some real family dysfunction, and all he could do was ask himself over and over, "What's going on around here, anyway?"

For Matt, the family secret was obvious. His mother and his grandmother were both drinking, certainly in an alcoholic manner (that is, drinking to get drunk). The fact that neither of them passed out or exhibited rowdiness didn't cancel Matt's painful awareness that this had been going on for years. It was what we came to call the "Saturday night ritual" in later therapy sessions.

When Matt realized that he was watching a replay of the day after such a Saturday night ritual, with his sister running in tears back up to her room and his younger brother behaving like a brat, then Matt knew that the family didn't *ever* talk about these nights of drinking. He further came to understand that apparently nobody had the courage to confront his mother and grandmother; they were the heads of the household, and that was that! So instead of getting the family secret out in the open, they just continued to play the charade over and over.

For Matt, the realization went even further. He came to understand that they really *hadn't* held a "special" dinner for him; this was what happened each and every weekend in this family home. Knowing this fact unlocked many things for Matt. He told me about some bizarre behavior: "I remember that when I was much younger and these drinking matches were really in high gear, I wanted to leave the house and go to visit my friends. But I couldn't."

"Why couldn't you get yourself out of the house, Matt? Surely, no one would have missed you if everyone was drinking as hard as you indicate."

"Simple. They took my shoes, and my brother's and sister's shoes, too!"

"What do you mean, *took* them?"

"Just what I said. My grandmother would order me to go to each of our rooms, get our shoes, and bring them to the living room where the 'party' was going on."

"Then what?"

"Then my grandmother tied all the shoes together and hung them from the chandelier over the dining table!"

"She didn't want any of you doing *what*, Matt?"

Matt connected with the therapy point I wanted him to see for himself: "My God! She didn't want any of us kids to *tell* the neighbors about the drinking that was going on!"

After he told me this, Matt sat back in his chair and took a long sip of his coffee.

"What are you thinking right now, Matt?" I asked.

"I'm just thinking that not a goddamned thing has changed back there!" he fairly spat back at me.

"And you're just now seeing it?"

"Not only am I just now seeing it, but I can't believe that nobody has done anything about it," Matt said.

Matt was getting some answers to the question "What's going on around here, anyway?" His own recovery program allowed him to step outside the family picture and have this particular family secret exposed to him in a clear and concise manner. He could remember years before, during and after his parents' divorce, when all the problems of the family had been placed on his father, who had "left" them, remarried, and was running a successful small business in another city.

What Matt learned now was that the divorce probably wasn't the basis for the family dysfunction and infighting. Rather, the source of the problem was the drinking, specifically the grandmother's drinking, which caused her to rant and rave at each and every member of the family and then the next day act as if nothing had happened. That was the real problem. That was what was "going on around here." Once Matt had identified the problem, he felt better.

Matt had wondered what exactly had made him not want to go home more often, finances notwithstanding. His mother and grandmother were constantly imploring him to visit more frequently, and he had felt reluctant. Being away from the home he grew up in had allowed him to block the memories of the Saturday nights that were bitter, resentful, hurting, and confining for Matt and his siblings. In the past, he had even laughed about the shoes being tied from the chandelier, passing it off as simply how "playful" his grandmother was.

More healing was in store for Matt when he was able to

identify the problem in his family. For years he had taken much verbal abuse from his mother and grandmother about his father because it was easier to blame Matt's father for everything that was wrong than face up to the problems themselves. Matt's father was not a heavy drinker of alcohol. The more Matt explored his childhood memories, the clearer it became that it was never his father who was drunk and abusive, but always the two dominant women in his life: Mom and Grandma.

Matt realized that his father had been taking a bad rap all these years and that his divorce had gotten him out of the situation. But Matt's mother and grandmother were trying to keep the focus of blame for everything that was wrong with the family, including Matt's own alcohol abuse, on Matt's father! By using Matt's father as the "heavy," this sick family was keeping the focus away from the real problem.

Matt is working now to try to get his sister and brother together to begin an intervention on both Mom and Grandma, seeking help for their alcoholism, which he is certain (as am I) has permeated this family. But before Matt could run any further on his track of getting well, he had to *identify* the problem.

We often tend to mask the real problems in our lives by shifting the focus away from ourselves and onto others. This is what the mother and grandmother were successfully doing. They kept having Saturday night bashes, getting inebriated, lambasting the husband/son-in-law who had "deserted" them, and then swallowing up the secret of their night's behavior right along with their morning orange juice and toast!

In order to identify the problem, the very first thing you must do is look at behaviors that seem to get repeated over and over. When certain family members get together, ask yourself, "Do these two *always* fight?" Look at the environment of the family when these problems occur. For Matt it was the Saturday night drinking; for you and your family it might be something far removed from that. It could be, for example, after church on a

Sunday morning. Look hard at the setting where these things take place. Ask yourself, "What makes this fight or argument happen *every* Sunday afternoon? Is there something that I'm missing about all this?"

Next, look at who is always involved in family upsets. Oftentimes there is a single "trigger" family member, who seems able to ignite whatever powder kegs are sitting around and whatever family members are sitting on those kegs.

Learn to identify the problem by "stepping outside" the family proper. A good, simple tool for you to use, one that I have my people in therapy use quite often, is making yourself take a step back—and observe. When a family problem has surfaced, or even is well under way in the form of arguments or tears, step away from it and say, "What's wrong with this picture?" Using that tool forces you to come to the next logical step, which is, "What needs to be done to make the picture right?"

This tool applies even if it is you who is right in the middle of the battleground. I know it's hard to do, but it's absolutely vital that you identify the problem by asking, "What's wrong with this?" and then, "What can be done to *correct* it?"

The answer is the final cap in your plan to identify the problem. You ask yourself or the others who are embroiled in argument or heated discussion, "What are we *really* fighting about here?" Just asking that question helps focus all of the participants on the real issue at hand and not on hidden agendas that may be creeping into the picture.

We are all very much aware that family fighting is not the only sign of a hurting family. Therefore, this approach applies to any problem situation. Use whatever tools will force you to identify the real problem. The problem may or may not be tied to a family secret, but the clues to problems often *are* in those secrets.

In this example of an argument that always seems to occur following church, the patient, Louise, couldn't for the life of her figure out what made her father and mother get into such bitter fights almost every Sunday following family worship. It wasn't until she learned that her father had once studied for the Jesuit ministry and left it to change careers that she got the clues. It was her family's secret that Dad had really never forgiven himself for leaving the calling to which he thought he had been committed. For him, church on Sundays was a very painful reminder of what he had done; it was not the serene and spiritually renewing process that one expects from attending church or temple.

Louise had been asked to identify what she thought the problem was in her family, and she had come up with the lame excuse that "Mom and Dad can't agree on the parish they want to be in." I asked her to step outside the picture and look at it objectively.

"Is that what is *really* wrong?" I asked.

We agreed on her plan to spend some time with her mother and father separately to try to probe the issue. Her father was pretty steadfast about his position of not liking the parish they attended, not caring for the sermons of the priest, generally not liking anything about the Mass because it was one of the new Masses that used no Latin and seemed untraditional.

When Louise confronted her mother on a separate occasion and asked, "What's gotten into you and Dad, anyhow?" she got a clue to identifying the problem in her family. Her mother told her, "Your father should never have married me. He should have just gone ahead and been a priest!"

Louise had known her father had gone to college and graduated. What the family had never discussed was that her father had been in seminary, studying for the priesthood, before meeting her mother, falling in love, and leaving his chosen profession and calling.

As soon as she knew this secret, Louise was able to identify the problem, and it had nothing at all to do with the parish, the priest, or the kind of Mass being said. When Louise became aware of the real problem between her parents, the three of them sat down (at her insistence) and got Dad to talk about his feelings at leaving the priesthood.

Louise said it was pretty painful because her father started to cry as they were talking. Even her mother had been unaware of the deep guilt that had overcome her husband, until the three of them started talking about it. Mom then began to assume some of the guilt, blaming herself for not "getting out of Frank's life," allowing him to finish preparing for the priesthood.

Before the situation was totally out of control, with everyone blaming one another, this fortunate group came into treatment as a family and worked through many of the issues that had caused so much upset.

Louise succeeded in getting the family secret out in the open. Even more important was that she learned that identifying the real problem—the one that sits behind the outward mask being worn by the family members—is the first step in going from hurting to healing.

Review the tools described in this chapter. Make it a point to practice stepping outside whatever is going on to ask yourself, "What's wrong with this picture?" Be prepared to follow up that question with the second part of the tool: "What will be necessary to make this picture right?"

You're preparing yourself to look at your family's hurting in a whole different way, a way that says it's going to be OK to talk, it's going to be OK to change.

Liken your quest for identifying family problems to looking for problems with your car. When you hear a funny noise that covers a whole lot of territory, maybe you have to lift the hood and narrow down the problem, identifying where the noise is coming from, but that's only a *part* of it. The important part is listening carefully to make sure that the noise is actually in the particular part itself, rather than simply sounding as if it's coming from there.

Maybe the noise is really being caused by something you can't readily see, something that's hidden beneath the wires and maze of accessories in your car's engine. It will be up to you or a mechanic (therapist) to finally trace the "funny noise" to the real culprit causing it. This is a process of diagnostic skill, and you will need to keep it with you as you explore the pages of this book, ever prepared to step out of the picture and begin asking, "What's going on around here, anyway?"

Identifying the *real* problem will be the first important step on your path away from family hurting to family healing.

4
Fixing the Responsibility

Now that you've had a chance to become a little more comfortable with the idea of a family secret even existing, it's time to look at a really sticky problem: which family member needs to "own" the secret. Just because everyone in the family knows about the secret and what the secret is doesn't mean that anyone has come racing forward, hands waving in the air, saying, "Yes! Yes! It's *my* secret, and I take full responsibility for it!"

Dream on! The very reason you feel the way you do is that this has not happened. Therefore, *you* have accepted the responsibility for the family secret, so *you* need to get the tools to rid yourself of the responsibility.

When you keep owning everyone else's responsibility because it's been driving you nuts that no one has come forward to take on the job for you, you are not helping the rest of the family, and you certainly are not helping yourself. This behavior, called *enabling,* has been a big factor in your not getting as well as you can get. By continuing to accept the responsibility for the family secret, you are allowing the person or persons who should own it to go scot-free.

Even if you think you have been helping all this time, it's high time that you take yourself out of that particular game and let the other folks jump right in. The problem that's been facing you all along is that no one has seemed willing to accept the responsibility. Of course, as long as *you* were willing, who was going to take that wonderful privilege away from you?

To make a change, begin with your first tool. Step outside the family picture for just a minute, and ask once again, "What's wrong with this picture?"

I like to call this "freeze-framing," from my old television and motion picture days. Imagine a picture of your family continually guarding the family secret, envision yourself taking the responsibility for that secret, and then freeze-frame the picture. Step outside and look back into the picture, watching yourself in the enabling actions that you have been doing.

When you have done that, you can reach out for the second tool that goes with freeze-framing. Ask, "What do I need to do to *change* this picture?" In other words, you are asking yourself, "Why am I doing this?"

Certainly, one of the answers is that you are enabling because there is some kind of payoff for *you*. You are getting some kind of emotional (and possibly physical) strokes out of your behavior. You are, in a word, continuing to accept the responsibility for the family secret because you get a direct need met. It could be a need that stems from your role in the family in the first place. If you have always been the "Chief Enabler" in the family hierarchy, then you continue in that role because it's second nature; you've been accepting the responsibility for the family behavior for years.

If you are the "Superhero," you are expected to accept responsibility for whatever anyone else in the family says or does. You've been led to believe that you've got some superpowers that can make everyone else well; all you have to do is continue to be the guardian of all their feelings and actions. No wonder you don't do anything to change that. You have a *lot* of power.

Suppose your role in the family has been that of the "Mascot"; if so, you can clown around with the family secret. You can continue to protect everyone from it by making jokes about it and taking the butt of the secret yourself, protecting the really responsible people from ever having to come forward.

If you fit into the "Lost Child" role in your family, then one of the ways you can call attention to yourself—getting the rest of the family to even *acknowledge* your existence—is to take all the weight of the secret upon your own shoulders, lifting the burden from the rightful owner(s).

These are just a few of the possible roles. Each carries its own rewards.

Tool three for you, then, is to acknowledge that you are getting some kind of payoff and decide that you don't need that anymore! It has just become habit for you to step right in and fix everything. At least you've *tried* to fix everything, and then when the fix didn't work, you kept blaming yourself and wondering what it was that *you* did wrong. If this sounds a lot like you, then it's time for some changes.

Getting the responsible family person to step up and take the responsibility may not be your job. What's important to remember is that this book is designed to help you free *yourself* from the hurting of the family secret.

Chances are, however, that when you step back into the picture you have been looking at, you will see more clearly who really needs to own the problem of the family secret. You have been in the way of seeing that clearly because it has been important for you to own the secret yourself, as part of the reward system you have set up for yourself.

Every time you have owned the secret, you have received a "brownie point" or two from at least two members of the family. The first stroke has come, probably with a silent look of gratitude, from the one who really should own the secret. The second stroking has come from whoever is left as the family head: mother, father, grandparent, older brother or sister. That person has given you a nod of approval because you have protected the real person and the secret, and thus you are protecting the family! That protection has become very important over the years. Whatever needed to be done, whatever new lies or conniving had to be done, *was* done, in order to keep the secret "safe" within the family!

The more you have acted to "save" the family secret, the more you have enabled the really responsible family member to continue denying his or her role in the family secret. So, all the time you thought you have been helping, you have really been hurting! Doesn't seem fair, does it?

Now we come to the most important tool of this chapter, the most important tool for you to use in extricating yourself from the position of being responsible and fixing the responsibility squarely where it belongs. Remember, this *doesn't* mean that you will succeed in actually getting the rightful owner of the family secret to step up and take the responsibility; it only means that you will pull *yourself* out of the way, clearing the path for that person to do what needs to be done. In this case, consider yourself the blocking halfback, taking out the rushing tacklers to allow your running mate to score. You are not carrying the ball, but simply preparing the pathway for the designated ball carrier.

Here's the tool: Unplug yourself from the family network. Imagine that your family is like a telephone switchboard, with a central operator—in this case, you—at the controls. Until now, when one family member has something to say to or *about* another family member—something that has to do with either the family secret or other sick behaviors of the family—*you* have been the one to take the message, interpret that message, and then pass it on to the family member for whom it was intended.

You can unplug yourself from that network by saying, for example, "Mom, I think that's something *you* need to take up with Brad! Here [imagine yourself moving phone plugs around on your switchboard], let me connect you with Brad!"

When you "unplug," you set up a direct connection between

the two family members (Mom and Brad), thus effectively taking yourself out of the family network. The net result is that Mom and Brad are going to have to talk to one another without you, the interpreter. It's just possible that one or the other of them will finally have to take responsibility for whatever is to be said or done!

For you, this is a great relief! Let me share an actual example of this from another case of mine.

It had been almost two years since the young woman, Cheryl, had spoken directly with her mother. Before the rift, they had been on the phone three or more times per week, just exchanging pleasantries and gossip and "female talk," as Cheryl put it to me.

"What happened between you and your mother?" I asked.

"I'll be damned if I know! She just got mad at me and wouldn't ever tell me what was wrong!" Cheryl replied. "I've asked my sister, but she can't get anything out of Mom either!"

"Do you talk often to your sister?" I inquired, seeking a possible link to what was happening.

"We don't talk as much as we used to . . . it seems as if we don't have much to say, except about what could be bothering Mom, and *she* doesn't know!"

We set up a family session, inviting Cheryl's mother, father, sister, and roommate. It didn't work. Not at first, anyway. Cheryl was reluctant to be the one to invite the rest of the family. After all, they didn't seem to care enough about her in the first place, so what would make me think that they would be interested in spending time with a *therapist*, for God's sake? (First clue: Mom doesn't believe in "therapists"!)

"Well, would you be willing to at least give it a try? Would you be willing to at least *ask*?" I pressed.

Not surprisingly, Cheryl replied, "I'd be willing to ask my *sister* to ask my mother."

"Good enough," I said, "let's settle for that, with the emphasis to your sister being on what a help this would be for *you*. Let's not suggest that the family will gain anything out of the session." It was my way of setting a small trap both for the patient and for the family.

The "secret" in this family was that Cheryl was a lesbian who had been in a female relationship for several years. The family had taken her "coming out" with apparent resolve and great calm—a lot of reassuring phrases and a lot of including the lover in family parties, dinners, and celebrations, as if they were a perfectly "normal" (as the mother later put it) couple. The problem was that all these actions reflected *surface* feelings. The secret of their daughter being lesbian was so well guarded that even the parents' closest friends didn't know.

So what had happened two years ago to blow things apart? Even though the mother knew of her daughter's sexual preferences, and even though Cheryl's family treated her roommate and lover as "family," Cheryl and her mother had never really sat down and talked about this. Everything went along smoothly until a friend of the family called the mother to complain that Cheryl was being "mean" to her at the place where Cheryl and the friend both worked. (Cheryl's father had pulled some political strings to get his daughter the job in the first place, largely through knowing this friend and calling in a favor he had done for her some years before.)

The mother confronted Cheryl—on the phone, of course—about what she had done to the family friend to be "mean" to her. Cheryl said she hadn't been mean at all; the woman was making some advances to her, advances she had naturally rebuffed for the sake of her relationship. The friend, not wishing to disclose her own lesbianism to the mother, had created a set of job-related incidents, which on the surface seemed to show my patient as being indeed mean, conniving, and downright back-biting to the fellow employee, particularly in talking of her to her supervisor. When Cheryl told her mother the truth of the other woman's sexual advances, her mother hung up on her!

From that moment on, since mother and daughter were no

longer in direct communication, guess who did all the interpret-
ing between them? The sister! She picked up the challenge and
finally felt *needed* again in the family, something she hadn't felt
for a long time. Not only did she talk to Mom frequently, picking
up the two, three, and four calls a week that used to be spent on
the other daughter, but she was the main connection about how
Cheryl was doing and so forth.

Naturally, Cheryl continued to wonder "what the hell was
bothering Mom" and continued to ask her sister what was going
on. The sister, Sharon, was now in the "switchboard operator"
position for the family and began to meet with Dad. This was
something that hadn't happened in a long time, and Sharon
savored the opportunity to get together with her father for lunch,
ostensibly to report to him on how Cheryl was doing.

So here were a mother and daughter who had been very, very
close, suddenly casting themselves further and further apart.
Every report back from either Dad or Sharon to Cheryl was,
"Mom is angry about your accusing their friend!"

Finally, using Sharon, I got a chance to meet with Dad, Mom,
Sharon, and Cheryl's roommate, Fran. Why Fran? She was the
"safety valve" member of the group. Mom wouldn't come to the
meeting unless Fran was included—Mom being convinced that
Cheryl was all to blame and that Fran would also be in Mom's
corner.

The session, to say the least, was strained.

"What's it like for all of you to be here in the same room just
talking with one another?" I asked as an opening gambit.

"Feels fine to me . . . *I'm* not the one who's mad!" Mother
volunteered—a strong clue that it was *exactly* she who was mad!

Mother was a domineering woman, and as the session cranked
up to full steam, I felt that she wanted to make peace but didn't
know how. Cheryl was dumbfounded by her mother. I asked
Cheryl to give her version of what had happened between them,
and Cheryl could only focus on the fact her mother had become
angry on the phone and hung up on her.

"I only hung up on you because you were lying to me about Helen [the family friend]! Why on earth would you make up something like that, Cheryl?" Mom fairly came out of her chair.

Sharon plugged right in to make things right, saying, "Mom! Cheryl! Can't we at least talk without *accusing* each other?"

I let them unload the rest of the "baggage." Dad remained silent, but Mom turned to Fran, putting her uncomfortably on the spot with, "Now, Frannie, *you* know I've never cared about how you and Cheryl carry on [her words], but to accuse *Helen* of being the same way is unthinkable!"

Aha! The family secret jumped out into the room for all to see and hear. Mom had no more accepted, understood, or worked through Cheryl's lesbianism in the more than three years since Cheryl's coming out than she had flown to the moon!

Everyone was suddenly *very* uncomfortable. Dad just cleared his throat, Fran looked helpless, and Sharon was fast loading up her emotional circuits with an outburst of her own, clearly showing she was taking responsibility for Mom and the family secret. She was unable to fix the responsibility for the falling out between her mother and sister where it truly belonged: with her mother and Cheryl.

"Mom, for God's sake!" Sharon fairly screamed, "Can't you let *that* alone, for once?"

Cheryl was angry as hell. She finally understood in one painful moment that her mother, and very probably her father, didn't understand her sexual preference at all; they had simply *tolerated* and buried their feelings about it, until it came dangerously close for them in the possibility that one of their friends had made advances to their daughter.

Sharon's body was racked with uncontrolled sobbing. It was just too much for her. She had been carrying the load for the family switchboard for too long and had not been able to unplug herself from the network, plugging in Cheryl and her mother directly to resolve the differences between them.

Helen wasn't the issue at all; in the long run, it didn't matter about Helen. The issue was that this family had a secret—their oldest daughter was a lesbian—and they had carried that secret around and around, stuffing it in their anxiety closet until it became dangerously in position to jump out at them.

After several more sessions, the family agreed to go out to dinner together, something they had not done for two years. Fran, on a cue from me, declined to go the first time, thus removing herself as a possible barrier to mother, father, and daughters talking about the lesbianism, something they should have done so long ago!

No wonder Mom hated therapists and therapy! She knew that sooner or later some therapist might open her closet door, and she just couldn't risk that.

Sharon entered some short-term therapy with a colleague of mine and was more than happy to give up her post in the family network!

Cheryl and her mother resumed twice-weekly phone conversations. Dad started having lunch regularly with each of his daughters alone, not needing either of them as a buffer between him and them. Fran spent a little less time as a "family member," keeping her relationship on a more clearly defined basis.

Fixing responsibility clearly upon Cheryl and her mother to resolve their differences and also getting them to talk openly, frankly, and in *loving* terms with each other about the "secret" of Cheryl's lesbianism was not possible as long as Cheryl's sister played the "operator." If you are an "operator," unplug yourself. As AT&T puts it so succinctly, it's really OK for all *your* family members to "Reach out and touch someone"!

That someone is each other—directly and without interference or garbled messages delivered from another family member to another family member. Fix the responsibility squarely upon the shoulders of the person who needs to feel it sitting there!

5
Assessing the Impact

How long have you been wondering whether your family secret is having any effect on your relationships with other people? Is there a subtle or perhaps not so subtle change in the way you are treated by your friends, neighbors, peer group, and co-workers?

You may simply brush all of the feelings aside and chalk them up to "paranoia," but chances are the feelings are real, not imagined. What makes this happen? People tend to "telegraph" their feelings; that is, we aren't as clever at masking our feelings in front of others as we may like to think.

How many times have you witnessed some sort of family argument—even some minor unpleasantness—then gone to work and tried putting on a happy face? Everything seems to be going your way until a colleague confronts you with, "What's the matter with *you*, for goodness' sake?"

There goes your mask! Your cover is ripped away, and someone has seen right through the brave front you have been advancing for all to see. Suddenly you may find your eyes welling up with tears, or you may suddenly develop sniffles that you want to attribute to "allergies" or "a slight cold." But you have telegraphed the feeling that all is not right with your world this day, and none of your alibis are going to save you!

The problems confronting you are obvious; you need to *tell* someone that there is trouble on the home front. But a dilemma arises if you are unable to share the family secret. You might alibi with: "Oh, it's nothing, really," or, "What makes you think something's *wrong*, for God's sake?" After such a response, you continue to feel miserable and very much alone because of the pickle you are in.

Fortunately, there are some tools you can use that will help ease your burden without requiring you to hang out all the dirty laundry. The way you use these tools may vary among the principal groups of people you encounter on most days: your friends, neighbors, and co-workers. Let's see if there are some better ways to assess the impact your family secret is having on you and these people.

Your Friends

If people are truly *friends*, you would think that they don't need an explanation; they probably know what's wrong in your family anyway. Well, that's not a safe assumption, and it really isn't fair to the friendship either.

Somehow friends tend to pick up on your moods even faster and more accurately than do family members; you can't or *shouldn't* try to fool them. So let them in on the fact that something indeed *is* wrong. You don't have to go for the Academy Award in doing this; just acknowledge that your friend is correct in assuming that something is wrong with you at home.

Now comes the assessment. It's important that you know what you are doing to telegraph your feelings. So, after acknowledging that all is not well, you say, "What am I saying or doing that makes you think there is something wrong?"

I call this getting to the hidden agenda. You've been going along thinking you are fooling everyone; then your friend suddenly pulls the mask away from your emotions, exposing the real, hurting you. Since you already tried to hide your feelings, you know you haven't done a very good job of it. Instead of defending yourself (that is, defending the agenda you presented for all to see), you need to get to the *real* agenda, the one you are missing. By asking someone else what you are presenting to the public at large, you get a real clue as to your own behavior.

Your friend might reply, "I always know when something's wrong, because of the way you hunch over when you walk," or, "You get that funny frozen smile on your face!" or, "When you start biting your lower lip like this [demonstrating], I know all is not well in paradise!"

If you just defend yourself by telling your friends that nothing's wrong, if you persist in carrying on with the charade, you will never find out what you are doing: the *hidden* agenda that your behavior is masking.

It is important to know what you are doing or saying—the exterior that you are presenting for all to see. If you know what behavior you are presenting, then you can *change* it! Getting well is all about changing behavior.

Now for the next part of the assessment. If your friend has pointed out something that you are doing or saying that is telegraphing your feelings, then you can plunge ahead with, "How is this affecting *you* [your friend]?"

It's important that you know how your friend is being affected by your behavior, because chances are that your casual acquaintances and even your enemies will also pick up on your telegraphing. Besides, this is your *friend*; this is someone special in your life who has always been there for you. Chances are that if you are hurting, then so is she or he.

Your friend's answer will help you focus on the solution to how you are behaving and make it easier to say whatever is bothering you at home. Your problem might have just been a simple argument that is related to the family secret, or it might be a major blowout. The point is that when you *acknowledge* that something is wrong, you are halfway to getting over the bad feelings!

Your friend may respond to your question by saying, "Well, when you are troubled, it affects me, because I care about you," or, "When you are hurting, so am I, and I don't *want* to hurt!"

The key to the assessment is for you to realize that it isn't just you who is affected by the impact of the family secret; everyone you contact can become affected, depending on you and your behavior. When you have made the assessment that it isn't just you who is reacting, then you can become even more determined to make the responsibility for the family secret fall on the proper shoulders as previously discussed. You begin to feel the impact on you and your friends, and it should make you angry!

You can then ask your friend for advice, whether you take it or not. This will help you hear someone else's point of view and allow you to focus even more on solutions to the problem, instead of focusing on the problem itself.

The mere act of being able to talk about the problem will reduce the anxiety that you are feeling *and* presenting by your behavior.

Your Neighbors

Many of your best friends may also be your neighbors. But for the sake of exploration, let's consider them as two separate groups. Your neighbors may be of the friendly yet nosy type. At least they may present themselves as nosy when they ask you, "Is everything OK with you, Jim?" or, "Say, Tammy, we haven't seen much of you lately . . . everything OK?"

Your first reaction to these kinds of questions is probably resentment. How dare these "strangers" inquire about you?

You may also feel that you have to be particularly on guard to protect the family secret from these neighbors, and *that* makes you even madder! But neighbors, like all problems, are not going to just go away because of your troubles. They require an answer, and once again, you need to be making an assessment of the impact your family secret is having on the neighbors.

The more flip you become in your reply, the more you just prolong the problem, since you are not going to be able to avoid your neighbors forever. The mere fact that they are inquiring after you is your biggest clue to the assessment. They have sensed that all is not right with you, so once again you must be telegraphing that feeling.

Use the same tools as those for use with your friend, but make this important change. The first thing to do is *thank* your neighbors for their concern. This acknowledges their feelings; it's helping validate their feelings that something might be wrong with you and that, far from being nosy, they want to *help*. You could say, "Oh, thanks for asking! Guess I *have* been absent around here the last few days . . . ."

Now, *acknowledge* the problem with something like, "We're having a little bit of a rough time right now, but I really appreciate your concern!"

The neighbors will probably ask whether there is anything they can do. Again, thank them and assure them that you will call on them if they can be of assistance to you.

What you have accomplished is to make and complete an assessment. You have assessed that the impact of the family secret is becoming more visible because your behavior is causing neighborly concern. You have not divulged the family secret, nor have you run pell-mell into the neighbors' homes and begged for help. You have simply had your eyes opened to the fact that there *is* an impact on people who live in your vicinity because they *feel* it and need validation of those feelings!

Neighbors are inclined to repeat their offers of, "Well, if there's *anything* we can do . . . !" and, "Be sure to call us first if you need help!"

This is OK. Just thank them, and don't try to turn them off.

They may be hoping that you will drop the tasty morsel of gossip about what's *really* happening behind your closed family doors, but you need to avoid this right now.

Remember, this problem might not even be your responsibility, so be sure not to suddenly own it just because the neighbor has found you vulnerable. This happens a lot. You are presenting or telegraphing vulnerability, so the neighbors jump right in to find out all they can, not so much from nosiness, but from the same sense of human kindness that makes neighborhoods what they are, communities of concerned people.

The biggest help in your assessment of the impact on your neighbors is to realize that if the neighbors are picking up on your feelings, then those feelings are pretty visible, and the family secret is affecting more than just you and your immediate family.

How is it affecting the neighbors? It is breaking set patterns that the neighbors are used to seeing, and the breaking of these patterns is causing concern. For example, a man who is generally seen driving into his driveway around five-thirty is not seen for a few days. He arrives Saturday morning from "someplace," his kids run out to the car, climb in, and away they go.

Neighbors seeing this conclude that "something's wrong at the Braxtons'." They have seen a break in a habit pattern; they draw a conclusion, whether it's correct or not, that "Bob Braxton must've moved out!" His wife's appearance on the scene later in the morning, looking hollow-eyed and acting edgy, confirms the belief that something is wrong. The impact of the family secret has now been felt by the immediate neighbors. The family didn't plan it that way, but that is how it works.

Thus, acknowledging concern expressed by the neighbors is important for *them*; it validates that everything isn't the same. Even if you are not ready to divulge the family secret, your neighbors have trusted their instincts based on seeing a change in set behavior patterns of you and your family.

It may be necessary to throw a "comfort blanket" on the situation, at least for now. The wife might say, "Bob is staying with his folks for a couple of days while we work out some problems." She makes the decision to confide even that much based on her assessment of the impact the noticeable change in behavior pattern has had on the neighbors. If they have become so used to seeing and perhaps greeting Bob Braxton every day, and then he has simply taken to driving up like a stranger and hurrying off without even stopping or going inside his own house, then this has affected the neighbors; they deserve a small explanation.

Peers and Co-Workers

Like your neighbors, your peers and co-workers may include some of your friends. For the sake of discussion, just assume that these groups are distinct and separate.

The impact your family secret may have on co-workers is further removed than it is from neighbors or close friends. Nevertheless, your co-workers are *directly* affected by your behavior, so that any visible signs of distress on your part affect them and *their* jobs, too!

Here's a case that happened early last year. An office worker was going through a rough time in her marriage. She and her husband had tried to keep the relationship together, but it was becoming obvious to everyone that Becky and Tad were not going to make it.

The business Becky worked for was an oil exploration company hard hit by the collapse of the energy boom. Some long-time employees had been terminated; others had been transferred to company branches out of state. The remaining employees were a pretty tight group of people, and when one person was visibly upset, all of them felt the backlash.

Everyone had heard Becky lament the sorry state of her marriage, and everyone was supportive of her. Supportive, that is, until one day Becky simply walked out of the office and out on her responsibilities.

When her supervisor called her, Becky said she was having a

rough time and was quitting for the day. This was not acceptable behavior, and it was putting the rest of the group in a terrible bind, since Becky was the principal word processor for their group. She had not given the company adequate time to replace her, and her absence was creating a critical logjam for the rest of the workers in her group.

They complained to the supervisor, saying this was beginning to be a habit with Becky; she had done this to them twice in the same month. As much as everyone was supportive of the woman and her personal problems, the supervisor made a decision to terminate Becky with a pretty nice severance check.

The office settled down with a replacement person for Becky, and things seemed secure until, lo and behold, the unthinkable happened. Becky was rehired by the company and given her old job back! This was extremely unsettling to the rest of the group, and the impact was so severe as to cause some open rebellion.

The company's willingness to take Becky back after the circumstances under which she left gave a clear enabling message to the rest of the workers. It was OK to let your family secrets (Becky's pending and rough divorce) interfere with the workplace. In other words, Becky's co-workers and peer group were directly affected by her behavior. They were even more affected by the *company's* behavior in sending a double message: "If your personal problem is rough enough, you can walk out on your job, and we'll probably take you back when you're ready to come back."

If you are being besieged by co-workers asking, "What's wrong?" and, "Is everything OK?" apply the tools described in this chapter. They will work for you, the more you use them! Here's how to use them in the workplace:

1. Ask, "What am I doing [or saying] to make you wonder if I'm OK?" (hidden agenda).
2. Ask, "How is this affecting you?" (assessing the impact).
3. Thank your co-workers for their concern (validating their feelings).

4. Assure them you will call on them if needed.

As you can see, a family secret affects more than just the family that is living and *protecting* such a secret. Your close friends, neighbors, and co-workers can all feel the fallout from this thing. The job that we have been discussing for you in this chapter is to learn to assess the impact your family secret is having on those around you.

You are reinforcing the growing conviction in yourself that *something* has to be done about this problem, that it is affecting more than just you and your family, and that the hurting you have been trying so valiantly to mask has come out in the open!

Your assessment of the impact may conclude, "It's none of his or her or their business, and I just don't give a damn!" However, that's probably not going to be the case and certainly will not help you break the isolation pattern that the secret has forced on you in the first place! The whole idea of this book is to help you get from the hurting to the healing, and having an "I don't give a damn" attitude won't help that process.

You *may* decide to disclose more or fewer pieces of information relating to the secret, based on the impact you believe it has caused. You will probably disclose more of the family secret to your closest friend than to any of the other groups. That's natural, but don't stop making the assessment on *any* of these people.

Finally, understand that the family secret will always have an effect like that of a stone dropped in a pool of water. The ripples that circle out from where the stone entered the water are far-reaching and will eventually engulf all the people who are anywhere near the center of the pool.

You use the tools for assessment of impact and act accordingly. In making this assessment, you will begin to feel more and more the necessity for change within yourself, freeing yourself from the web that the family secret has spun around your own shoulders—a web that has trapped you in the "hurting" stages of your life.

6
Offering Solutions

"**I** simply don't know *what* to do!"
"Where does anyone get help, anyhow?"
"I feel *totally* helpless to change anything!"

You've doubtless thought or uttered one of these statements if you've become a victim of family secret-keeping. There *is* help out there—plenty of it! The biggest stumbling block is *you*. You are a stumbling block if you keep putting off making the offer of a solution to the sickness that has prevailed in your family.

Most people, particularly those I am privileged to work with as a therapist, have a basic flaw in problem solving. They spend a lot of time and energy in focusing on the problem, when they should be spending their energy on the solution! Now that we are five chapters into this book, it's time to turn from the *problems* of family secrets to some *solutions*, and thus move closer to the "healing" side of the ledger.

If you have been following the plan—if you have identified the problem, then fixed the responsibility squarely where it belongs—you are ready for this next vital step, that of offering solutions, either for yourself or the other responsible family member.

This chapter discusses three elements of help: individual therapy, family therapy, and self-help groups. One, two, or all of them will fit your case.

Individual Therapy

Many people are terrified of the idea of entering the process we call therapy. What is the reason for this fear? There are many, of course, but probably the most singular fear is the idea of *disclosing* so much about yourself to a stranger. Unfortunately, this kind of thinking simply perpetuates the family secret. After all, if you can't even tell a trusted professional in *confidence*, how are you ever going to expand the secret-telling process so that *all* family members can benefit from bringing the secret into the light of day?

So if you are afraid of working with a therapist, you must overcome this fear. Try confiding in a friend who has taken advantage of the therapy process. Ask him or her how it felt to begin in therapy and see if your friend will recommend his or her therapist to you. When you talk to your friend, you need not discuss your family secret. Rather, confide your desire to "talk to a professional."

Your minister, priest, or rabbi also will have a list of sources you can use to find a therapist with whom you will be able to work.

In your local telephone directory, you will find plenty of listings for treatment centers, treatment programs, psychotherapists, psychologists, and counselors. Your local, county, city, or regional mental health association is an excellent source of referrals.

Some therapists will charge you based on your ability to pay. Others will be covered by your health insurance for as much as 50 or 80 percent. Some insurance policies will even cover these costs totally.

Your mental health is important—equal to your physical health. You should choose your therapist with the same care as you would use in selecting your personal physician (who, by the way, is another excellent source for referral to a therapist).

I have purposely excluded the listing of psychiatrists from your selection choices at this time. Initial assessments made by competent therapists will help determine whether the more intense methods of a psychiatrist are called for. An example would be instances calling for the prescribing and monitoring of medications to help with certain anxiety disorders.

The next question that usually crosses a person's mind is whether the therapist should be male or female. This debate will rage on for whole bunches of time, depending on who you ask. My recommendation is to look at the *problem* facing you. It might be very difficult, for example, for you to work with a male therapist if you are female and concerned about sexual issues such as rape, incest, abortion, or sexual addiction. On the other hand, maybe you would feel more at ease in working with a male on such problems as alcohol abuse and other chemical dependencies. The operative word for you in making this selection is *comfort*.

If you are not put at ease in your first session with the prospective therapist, if you don't feel that there will be a good working relationship between the two of you, then tell him or her that you wish to look around. The therapist won't be offended; most therapists will operate the way we do at our Gateway Treatment Center and *encourage* you to shop around and look at several different people or places. We don't want a prospective patient spending all his or her time getting over the mechanics of personalities, instead of working on the real problems.

Once you have found a therapist, what will individual therapy do for you? It gives you the opportunity to explore the terrible feelings that are nagging at you, those feelings that you can't pinpoint but that just keep controlling your life. Therapy will assure you that you aren't "crazy" or unique; millions of people are suffering from the same things that brought you to the therapist in the first place.

Therapy of any kind will offer you choices; you have to do the work, but therapy will show you that there are *other* ways that lives can be lived besides the way in which you are living yours.

One of the most valuable tools of therapy is the knowledge that a patient can share his or her problems in *confidence,* that this person listening will walk the paths of recovery together with the patient, and that the patient does not have to feel alone with the problem again!

Individual therapy will lead you into a more firm position on the true identity of the problem, as well as help you confirm your thoughts about on whose shoulders the responsibility for the problem should rest. Even though you have already been trying to arrive at the answers to those questions, in therapy you will get *validation* for those answers. If you've been heading down an incorrect path, you and your therapist can and *will* explore new ways for you to go!

Family Therapy

Another solution for your consideration is family therapy. Once you have engaged in individual therapy, family therapy will become a natural extension of the get-well process. The next chapter provides some ideas for how to get the family into therapy.

What family therapy will do for you and the others involved is help you share the burden for the family secret, no matter who has been identified as the prime carrier of the secret.

Family therapy will also allow everyone to speak his or her mind in a safe environment. I can't stress this point enough! One of the reasons the family secret has been perpetuated is that no one in the family has ever felt *safe* to talk about it. The fear of family reprisal is so great that all the family members hold their tongues, but in a family therapy setting, the therapist offers the safe haven for talk that the family needs.

The other major point of family therapy is that the therapist will keep the sessions appropriate, so that they do not simply become unbridled "cut sessions" (insults for the sake of hurting not helping) at one or more members. Yes, there will be tears, gnashing of teeth, swearing, and maybe even some stomping out of the room, but it will be worth it! Trust me.

Many times family therapy will be the means by which individual persons will enter their own private therapy to continue working on specific problems. A good example of this is a family who may be dealing with a closeted drinking problem of one of the family members. While the structure of the family therapy may center around how this drinking is affecting the rest of the family and how, either through confrontation such as crisis intervention or some other means, help is obtained, therapy sessions nevertheless can springboard other family members into seeking individual help for other problems.

Many times other members of a family session have sought help from me for individual problems that have arisen as a result of the thrust of the family therapy sessions. The general rule for us is that I will refer them to a colleague if I feel that my work with the family as a whole might be compromised by seeing any of the members individually.

On the other hand, in some situations it might work perfectly well for one therapist to see individual members and *still* work with the family as a whole. Recently, I was brought to California to work with a family on a possible crisis intervention for an alcoholic family member. Obviously, the cost to the family and the distance involved made it prudent to try to get as much mileage as possible out of the few short days.

Therefore, as a perfectly workable plan, I spent several hours with the entire family as a group, focused on the problem of the drinker and the details of the intervention. In between, we scheduled individual therapy sessions for each member of the larger group, in which the individuals could share other concerns with me as their "on-site" therapist. They were a wonderful family, and as a result of our individual sessions coupled with the family sessions, some of the members have entered ongoing work with professionals in their various hometowns, helping them resolve some of the problems that we uncovered together.

Family therapy means a solution for help around the devastation caused by the family secret. It becomes a safe manner in which each family member can express an opinion, receive constructive feedback, and plan changes that will start building healthy family relationships.

Self-Help Groups

Because self-help groups provide support for you, they have a very definite place in the healing process. The problem is that they are not designed for, nor do they contain the framework to deal professionally with, the seriousness of family secrets and the aftermath a secret can cause. Such groups, therefore, should never be a substitute for treatment.

Of course, you will always find circumstances and cases where people "got well" strictly by using self-help, people who have not relied on treatment centers and professionals, effectively using instead the doctrines of the self-help group. One cannot, for example, fault the tremendous success rate of an organization such as Alcoholics Anonymous, whose thousands of members owe much of their sobriety to the work of that organization. On the other hand, within the framework of a self-help group, problems so often arise that cannot be dealt with effectively, because there is no trained professional monitoring the emotions and keeping the situation from escalating out of control.

One time, I was asked to speak to a self-help group about the effects of alcoholism on the family. It was a well-attended meeting, and when I was finished, a woman came up to me to thank me for the lecture. "This has been a big help to me in understanding the problems between my husband and me," she told me.

I asked her the status of her marriage, and she replied, "Oh, we're separated."

"I'm sorry to hear that," I said. "How long have you been separated?"

"Going on *eight years!*" she said, almost as a badge of courage.

Well, this woman wasn't too interested in getting well, in my opinion, since it was obvious that she was using her self-help group simply to hide from the methods and ways that she and her husband might work on their problem together!

When you seek or find a self-help group, it's important that you don't just hide within the group. So often, people will faithfully attend meetings of their group but sit in a corner of the room and *never* participate!

Obviously, this isn't doing either them or the group one bit of good. If you fall into that trap, you will just be lost forever, going nowhere on the path from hurting to healing!

Use your group as a sounding board, seeking feedback from people who are or have gone through the same or similar problems. But be careful! Don't ask or expect the group to provide treatment for you. Seek instead the comfort in knowing that you are definitely not alone and that your participation in such a group is ample evidence of the comrades who are yours.

Participating in a self-help group is a good solution for another reason; it will often break the ice for you in the tricky business of dealing openly with your feelings. And in that regard, there is no substitute!

There's also the matter of money to be considered. Perhaps you simply cannot afford professional treatment of any kind; maybe you live in a community that offers no mental health treatment, or for whatever other considerations, the self-help group is the only choice.

Then, for goodness' sake, *use* it! I can think of nothing more terrible than knowing you are trapped with a family secret that is eating away at you and also knowing that there is a self-help group just down the way that's available but going unused by you! That would suggest that you simply are not interested in breaking out of the chains that are binding you, that you have become used to the miserable life you are leading!

That's sad, isn't it? Understand that *help* is the key word—help for you in the best form that is available.

The *ideal* solution would be to obtain some kind of professional help *first* and then to use self-help as a dynamite combination for what you can term "aftercare" for the problem. This is a way to reinforce the tools that you will receive through this book and whatever other professional help you get. The use of the tools will keep you from falling back into the same old traps; it will keep you invested in the process of staying well, not only now, but for the future.

That is what healing is all about! It is a *process*, and anything that aids that process—anything and everything that keeps it moving—is what you are after. Therefore, explore the solutions discussed in this chapter. Think them through and talk about them.

You will generally not be charged for the first assessment session that you obtain with a private therapist, and public health organizations will schedule an appointment with one of their staff at no charge or on the basis of your ability to pay. Of course, self-help groups do not charge anything; freewill contributions can be made for the general upkeep of the group, but you are under no obligation. In other words, there is really *no excuse* for you not to pick up one of these solutions and run with it!

In this chapter we have talked about ways in which you can get help from individual and family therapy and self-help groups. You need to have been talking to treatment programs and centers and exploring self-help groups based strictly on *your family needing help*. That is, from the very beginning you should be disclosing to either a treatment program or individual therapist or someone who is going to help make the assessment around the real issues that you are seeking family treatment. The individual treatment that can come out of family treatment will fall naturally into place as you and the others feel the need, perhaps, to continue on an individual basis with help for yourself after a certain amount of family work. Obviously you're not going to try to take your entire family to a meeting of Alcoholics Anonymous, but how about attending groups for adult children of alcoholics and, where appropriate, other programs that will be available at the mental health or treatment facility that you have selected?

A good case in point is a couple I saw who had suffered the loss of an infant granddaughter. Everyone had waited for so long for the baby to be born and had, of course, lavished much love and care on the child when she did arrive. But the baby had a congenital heart defect, and she was struggling from the very beginning. The baby lived for several months, never quite well but garnering into herself the love and devotion of her parents, siblings, and grandparents, who were so proud of their "baby girl." Inevitably, the infant died, and the entire family was struck with grief.

I was seeing the grandparents as a couple in marital therapy for their own relationship problems, and it was obvious that they could not move beyond the grief they were feeling not only for their daughter and her husband who had lost the child, but also over another issue that had come to light: They were not being given a chance to grieve openly. The parents had determined that there would be no memorial service, no burial, no funeral. Instead they had the baby's body cremated, and the parents took the ashes to the mountains without anyone else present and spilled the ashes into one of the mountain streams where they had taken the baby on an outing during the summer.

The grandparents simply did not know what to do with their grief. They knew that they were a generation removed from the loss, and yet it was devastating to them that there was not a way for them to openly express this loss. They felt they had to be strong for the daughter and son-in-law, and yet it seemed as if those two had little or no regard for these two wonderful people who had also suffered an enormous loss.

It was suggested to them that they needed to be attending grief therapy, and indeed they did! They discovered that the hospital in which the baby had been born was offering a day-long seminar in grief therapy for those who had suffered such losses. The grandparents, much to their reward, entered the program to go through the one-day grief therapy sessions along with the parents. It was exactly what I had hoped for. Now they would have a chance to openly express their grief with other people who had suffered the same loss. This was a terribly important part of the getting-well process.

Later, these two people were able to share with their own couples group how important it had been for them and what a healing process it had been to go to a grief therapy group. It had not been very expensive (less than $75, as I recall, for the entire day), and it had been valuable for them in learning how to cope with their sorrow and how to help their daughter and her husband do the same.

As this case illustrates, it is important to find the right group, the one that will give the family the most help. Locate a place, person, or persons who specialize in family therapy—particularly those who understand the keeping of and feeding upon a family secret as a means of keeping a family sick.

If you are finding yourself stuck with the decision to seek help, then go back to some of the tools you have already learned to use:

- "What's keeping me from taking any action here?"
- "What do I need to do to make this change?"

If you can honestly face the answers that will come back to you, then you are on the right track. If you keep putting off even asking yourself these questions, then it's a pretty good sign that you are becoming even more comfortable with your sorry state of affairs.

If you're good and angry with me by now, that's healthy! This book should goad you into looking at making changes, changes that will benefit you in the long run. I can't make the decision for you; only you can pick up on one of the solutions and try it out. You have nothing to lose except your anger and frustration, and you have absolutely *everything* to gain!

7
Handling Objections and Put-Offs

Now that you have considered solutions in the form of using individual therapy, family therapy, and self-help groups as a way for everyone in the family to handle the bugaboo of the family secret, you face one of the toughest tasks: that of handling objections and put-offs to get started. You will now run into a situation where it's important that you be a master at parrying all of the objections that are going to be advanced from family members and from the person who may be the subject of the family secret. This chapter offers you some new tools that can make you a master of strategy in handling these objections to a family getting well.

You may be asking, "Well, why wouldn't my family want to get well?" Resistance is perfectly natural; after all, who wants to get well when staying sick is such an easy task! It isn't so much that the family doesn't want to get well; it's that the family doesn't recognize that it is as sick as it is. Also, getting well is going to take a lot of effort, and the family has been so used to operating in a sick environment that doing so has become second nature. As a matter of fact, it's become such a second nature that to operate in a well environment would seem abnormal.

If this seems strange to you, look around at your own situation. How many times do you see the family continuing to behave in exactly the fashion they always have, as in the examples we've been looking at in this book, and not doing anything to change? It's much easier to stay in the trap of the old ways than it is to take a risk and examine the new ways through which you could break out of that trap. So try to accept the fact that your family, and probably *you*, don't want to change.

In handling objections from family members, the first thing you need to do is to *separate* the family members. That is, don't try to deal with the family as a group, but rather begin to deal with them on an individual basis. That gives you the opportunity to be in much more of a command position than if you were setting yourself up against all of them.

Indictments

The first tool that you can use may sound kind of harsh; I call it "the indictment." The word *indictment* is kind of scary in itself because it's something you might hear in a trial or when the IRS comes knocking at your door. Well, in a way it is like that, because in order to handle the objections and put-offs from your family members, you'll have to create a list of all of the situations in which keeping the family secret has been harmful. *That* is what I mean by "indictment."

I have thought for a long time of another word that would fit, but *indictment* is a word I often use in doing crisis intervention around alcohol and drug abusers, where all members of the intervention party are involved in remembering dates, places, facts, and figures in which the person who is the subject of the intervention has been involved and where his or her use of alcohol or other drugs has caused an embarrassment or a disastrous situation. Over the years, the term *indictment* just seems to fit the bill. So let's stick with it and use it as a tool for you.

Your list of indictments, then, needs to be broken down into obvious situations where each individual family member has been involved and where the family secret has been the real culprit in keeping the family in a state of unwellness. That's why it's important for you to break down the family members into individuals so that you're dealing with them on a one-to-one basis.

Let's say it is your mother who is the first one of your "victims" for dealing with the family secret. You would sit down quietly and alone and, over a period of time (whatever period of time is necessary for you), recall and write down the events by date and place as best you can remember where your mother was involved in protecting the family secret in a particular situation, and how painful it was for you. Going back to Chapter 3's example of an alcoholic mother and grandmother, that event would be recalled with words such as, "Do you remember the weekend I came home to visit, and you and Grandma got very drunk?" Then you continue, event by event, very much as if you're taking inventory on each member of the family as you're doing this. After you have listed all your indictments, try to organize your list so they have some chronological order.

The second important part of the indictments is to write, and be prepared to share, how each of these events affected you. What's important in handling objections and put-offs is to be certain that all persons involved understand that their actions have contributed to your feeling bad, and that you are prepared not to have this happen anymore.

Some indictments you will throw out upon rereading them and further examining whether or not the family secret was really involved. That's where you have to be quite judicious. Don't make this an opportunity for one mammoth "cut session"! This is not the time for you to dump all the garbage that you've been carrying around for years and years. So weed out any issues that have little or no bearing on the family secret, and stay with the impact of the family secret on your life and the life of your family.

Once you have prepared the indictments on a family member, the next step is to figure out the best way to present them. As in the intervention technique, you shouldn't do this in the "blanket security" of the family home. There are a lot of reasons for this. One is that it's too easy for the person who has to sit down and listen to these indictments to simply say, "I've had enough of this garbage," and leave the room, which leaves you holding the bag!

So you might have to spend a little money and take Mom to lunch! Actually, in any public place where there is *some* privacy, such as a nice restaurant or just over tea in a café where it's fairly quiet, you can be fairly unobtrusive at a corner table. The reason for choosing such a location is that as you begin to present these indictments, they are going to open up some wounds, and they will probably unleash some protest, particularly from the person who is being "forced" to listen. But, because you're in a public place, the chances of the person creating a spectacle and causing any kind of an uproar are very slim. That gives you the opportunity to continue to present the list. And that's really your purpose. At this stage, you simply want to get the family member to listen to what you have to say.

The next part of your indictment presentation is to make sure that you are not attaching blame per se. That is, it's important for you to handle your indictment by saying things like, "Mom, I was so embarrassed last Christmas Eve when . . . , but," you continue, "we *all* fell into the same trap. Did you notice that *nobody* said anything about the way Jim was behaving?"

When you're doing this, you are including yourself as part of the family that has continued to be part of the network of sickness that has kept the family secret alive and flourishing. And that's much different from handing Mom all the blame and saying, "Why didn't *you* do something about this?" or, "This never would have happened if *you* would have taken charge!" So you want to avoid, in the indictment, any kind of personal responsibility.

It might be important for you to act as a mini-interventionist in this. That means that you're asking the person to whom you are talking simply to listen to you. Say things like, "Please just listen to what I have to say, and I'll listen to what you have to say when I'm finished," or, "Please, Mom, this may be hard for you to hear, but it's really important for me to be able to say it to you, so please don't interrupt until I'm finished." What you're trying to do is, on the one hand, put the person you're talking to at ease and, on the other hand, make sure that person is going to listen to what you have to say.

Now you've come to the delicate part. After the indictments have been presented, you have promised the family member an opportunity to respond. The first thing that's going to happen is that the person is going to *deny*. You'll hear things like, "Oh, really, Joyce, that didn't have anything to do with what really happened!" or, "I can't *believe* that you think all of this is directly tied in to [the family secret]!"

That's OK. Denial is a normal part of the process, and you should expect it. What you need to do is be prepared to handle it. And the way you handle it is by simply saying, "Mom, you don't have to be defensive about this! No one is accusing you."

This may seem hypocritical. Aren't the indictments all about accusing? Well, not exactly. You're *presenting* the indictments, but you're not acting as judge and jury, which is why the term *indictment* is so apropos. In a court of law, an indictment is a statement of fact and the basis under which the charges are being pressed. The person who is presenting the indictment will not be the person who decides the guilt or the innocence. Thus, your job is simply to present the indictment, pointing out to Mom or whichever family member you're working on at the time the list of situations in which the family secret has become involved.

The clincher to all of this, of course, needs to be, "What can we do about it?" And that is where you have to be prepared to say, "We need help!"

You may feel that if you do this, you're going to be the

laughingstock of the entire family. And that's a possibility! But isn't it worth it? Aren't you tired of continuing along the way things have been? If you are, you need to be willing to take a little of the scorn that may come your way for presenting these ideas. That's what I mean about taking risks to make changes.

Plan of Action

The next step in the process of working with the individual family members and their objections and put-offs will be for you to offer a specific plan of action. It won't do any good for you to say, "We need help," and then be unwilling to come up with what the family can do about it! You should have already made some arrangements for an appointment with a therapist or with a group where you can begin to get an assessment of the problem, as we discussed earlier. Simply present that plan to the family member you are talking to. You could say something like this: "I'm asking that we go see [therapist] about this problem. The therapist has given us an appointment for Wednesday evening at seven-thirty." Or, "Mom, I feel so strongly about this that I've taken the liberty of making an appointment with a therapist for us to just talk."

At this point, you're going to get the objections, all the excuses in the world, most of which you've heard before, but a lot of them will be new to your ears. These are going to be objections such as, "*I'm* not washing the family laundry in front of a stranger!" or, "You've got to be kidding!" and, "We don't need a therapist. We can solve our own problems!" If you think these responses are farfetched, just insert your own family members and imagine that you have gone through such an indictment session. Imagine what their put-offs and objections would be.

Here is another example that might be closer to home. How many women do you know who are staying in miserable, absolutely unproductive marriages or relationships based on the fact that "our family has never had a divorce before"? That particular objection keeps many women locked in and unable to move, paralyzed with the mere elements of something that hasn't happened before and their conviction that they shouldn't be the ones to make any change or take any risk!

As you can see, you're going to get plenty of objections. So how do you handle them? First of all, it's important that you hear them out. Second, be prepared to offer an alternative. If you have proposed visiting with a therapist at seven-thirty on Wednesday, Mom might offer an objection to that by saying, "You know that my Wednesday evenings are tied up with the Altar Society." You need to come back immediately with an alternative to the objection, and this is something you will have been able to work out with the therapist or with the self-help group that you have been in touch with. Your dialogue would go something like this:

"Mom, I've made an appointment with the therapist for Wednesday evening at seven-thirty just to talk about the problem."

"Well, you know I can't go on Wednesday evening at seven-thirty even if I wanted to, because that's when the Altar Society meets!"

"Well, Mom, the therapist can also see us Friday during the lunch hour or Thursday evening at eight. Which would be more convenient for you?"

What you've done here is use a valuable professional sales tool! Any professional salesperson can tell you that the way he or she handles objections and put-offs is to be prepared to answer the objections with alternatives. In this case, you are offering alternative times. You could also offer alternative places.

You can apply the same approach to self-help groups and say, "Well, Mom, this group also meets on Saturday mornings at nine and Sunday evenings at five. Which would be more convenient for you?"

The idea is that you don't have all your eggs in one basket. You have alternatives so that it's very difficult for the person offering the objection to weasel out. By the way, when you are talking to the therapist you have contacted, make sure that you do get several times that are available. Then be sure to confirm one of those times so that you don't keep the therapist hanging with a lot of empty spaces to fill. Most therapists will be able to give you a fairly wide range of times because they're anxious to be of service to you and want to be as accommodating as their schedule will permit.

If the family member persists in saying that none of those times work, go back to restating the indictment list. This time, do it a little differently. Say things like, "Mom, I am simply *not* going to go through another Christmas like the last!" or, "Mom, unless we're going to do something about this, you can count me out for the next birthday party!" Whatever the indictments have been on your list, you get the idea. You simply go back and restate them and reemphasize, adding this time a consequence: your lack of participation in whatever the family function may be, even if it's going out to dinner. You are saying that you are not going to continue to be a part of this sickness, and you're relying on the fact that the family members want you to remain a member of the family and therefore might give in to your simple request.

This is a good time to suggest that there's going to be no charge for the assessment, so they really "have nothing to lose, and *we* have everything to gain!" That is an important point. You're asking for a family member to spend fifty minutes to an hour in simply being able to get an assessment on whether or not there can be some help for the family around the family secret. It's not going to cost anything! Of course, therapy or continuing treatment *is* going to cost, but self-help groups—if that's where you end up—won't cost you any more than a freewill contribution if you want to make that.

What is required of you is persistence. You have to be prepared to handle the objections and put-offs by offering enough solutions that one of them is certain to work.

The solutions really just get you in to begin the talking process; they're not really solutions to the family secret, and you shouldn't present them that way. This is a good time for you to show some humility on the subject. You can say things like, "Mom, I'm not sure this is going to work, but it's sure better than where we have been!" Or, again going back to the idea of having nothing to lose, you say, "Mom, I *know* there is a better way! We simply need to have someone point us in the right direction." And then you always use the follow-up clincher: "You need to hear me, Mom; I am *not* going to continue living my life this way . . . it's just too painful!"

Well, I've been picking on poor old Mom, but the idea will apply to any family member. And you can see, if you were trying to present indictments to more than one family member, they would all be banding together, and *you* would be the bad guy! So be sure that you keep family members separated while you're presenting the indictments.

At the conclusion of your session, it's a good idea to say, "By the way, Mom, I'm having lunch tomorrow with Jim [brother], and I'm going to do the same thing with him that I've been doing with you today." You should proceed to tell her that you have arranged to meet each and every family member, that this will require some work on your part, and that it will mean you will have done your homework and will have gotten definite appointments with each family member to present this information.

This process may sound like a lot of work. And it is! Getting well is going to require some work, and staying sick is very easy to do. So you have to decide the risks.

But how much time and energy and work have you put into *avoiding* all of these issues, and how long has your family secret been affecting your family and yourself? When you begin to weigh the possible good that can come (and the probability is in *your* favor), then the time, effort, and energy that you're putting into this will be well worthwhile! When you consider the alternative is staying sick, it doesn't seem like such a bad investment.

Look at the tools of the indictment as a means to be able to do two things: (1) to get your *own* thinking more clearly into focus about exactly what the family secret has done to affect your life, and (2) to keep you organized so that your presentation of the facts and data to the family members will show that you are truly concerned—so concerned that you have taken the time to organize your thoughts and to present them in a fashion that shows the importance of it to your life. That's the main reason for spending quiet time by yourself to make up this list. Taking your own inventory first will help make you healthy, and then you will be more prepared to help take the inventory of other family members at least as far as the indictments are concerned.

Indicting the Subject of the Secret

Handling the objection or put-off from the person who may be the subject of the family secret works basically the same way as with other family members. There is one special exception. The person you're talking to *is* the family secret! I say that with all due respect, not to point out this person is some kind of freak. Because this person or an act committed by this person is the basis of the family secret, he or she needs to be treated a little differently. In the same setting as you used with other family members, you need to present a secondary list of indictments.

You may be saying, "Oh, no! I have to write *another* list?" Well, not exactly. Take the same list of indictments, but put it in a secondary position by saying to the subject, "You know, Jim, what happened last Christmas could have been avoided, and I really felt sorry for you going through that situation and having all of us ignore it!" Such a remark alludes very strongly to the incident of the indictment. Let's say that brother Jim had too much to drink at the family gathering around the Christmas tree, and that all the family members had ignored this as they have done so often before, never really recognizing Jim's drinking problem. (I'm using alcohol here because it's an easy one to use for this kind of situation, but the same approach is just as easily workable for a seizure that has been occurring frequently but no one talks about it outside the family. Or it could be any number of situations where the person who is the family secret acts out that secret to the embarrassment, but *closeted* embarrassment, of the rest of the family members.)

After taking the blame for your part in not doing anything about the incident, you continue by saying, "I think it's time we got some help with this. What do you think?" Well, for sure Jim is going to dig in his heels and take a firm stand and say things like, "I don't *need* any help," or, "Why don't you just mind your own business?" You need to be prepared once again to say, "If you don't need any help, why haven't you done something about it? I'm asking *you* to help *me* deal with this issue, because it's affecting me!" This helps to take some of the pressure off the family member and focuses on the fact that the family secret can no longer be ignored, at least by you.

If the family member still objects after you have presented times in which you have arranged an assessment session, then you may have to get into a small threatening position. I emphasize the word *small*. You can say things such as, "I had hoped that you would be willing to help me with this, Herb. But since you're not, you need to know that *I* am going to go ahead and keep the appointment, because I need help, and I am no longer going to be able to keep this family secret!"

Now the cat's out of the bag! You're saying that you are offering the opportunity for help to all family members, including the subject of the secret him- or herself, but if they are not going to accompany you, *you* are going to go ahead and divulge the family secret for your own well-being!

"Traitor!"

"How can you *do* this to us!"

"You just *wait!* I'll get you!"

You need to have the courage of your convictions, and that

courage leads you to say, "Look, folks, I'm offering *us* the opportunity to get well as a family. But if any of you don't want to do this, I absolutely have to proceed for my own well-being!"

So far, you've been dealing with individual family members, but now you can count on the family members coming together and comparing notes. And, in order to protect the family secret, they're going to make *you* the scapegoat. They're all going to say that it's *you* who has the problem and not them. But you're counting on the fact that someone will at least humor you and agree to keep an appointment for help, or attend a meeting with you.

That's all it takes! One chink in the armor of that protective family, and you have begun to win the battle. It may not seem that way to you, and it may seem like a long and slow process, but remember, you and your family have spent quite a long time getting sick and staying sick. So aren't you willing to devote a little time and energy to getting well?

Again, it's very important for you to maintain the courage of your convictions. Those convictions are that life has become intolerable, at least a portion of it, due to the family secret, and that you're not comfortable staying that way any longer. This conviction makes it much easier for you to continue on in the face of the resistance you will encounter from family members.

Some of them will surprise you. Some of them will say, "I've known that we've needed to get help for a long time," and, "Thanks, Jan, for taking the bull by the horns!" You will find some divisiveness for sure, and there will be some choosing up of sides, "them" against "us." But that's OK. Eventually the family will get together, as we'll see in the coming chapters, and eventually they will be prepared to at least listen to one another, something they, in all probability, have not been doing for some time.

There is another special side to the person who is carrying the responsibility of the family secret. When you're talking to him or her, you want to be in a position of offering comfort with such words as, "I know how hard this has been on you, Jim," or, "Jim, I see no reason for you to continue to go through this thing alone," or, "Jim, haven't you often wished you could just *tell* someone about this problem?" Finally, the clincher is, "Jim, there is absolutely no reason for you to be *afraid*! I love you and care about you, or I wouldn't be willing to put us through the initial pain I'm sure this will cause."

What you've done with these comments is acknowledge the fact that it's tough on the person carrying the burden of the family secret, particularly if he or she *is* the family secret. But you're also saying that you're right in there with him or her, and that you're doing this out of love, care, and concern, not out of some kind of desire for revenge because he broke your favorite doll when you were kids or he stole all the marbles! Remember that if the process of getting sick is one of dysfunction, the process of getting well is one of love.

If objections and put-offs continue to come from the main subject, go back to your old standbys:

- "What do we have to lose?"
- "Don't you think it's time we all faced up to this?"
- "This is really *important* to me!"
- "I think we have been a sick family too long. Don't you think we deserve a chance to get well?"

Get the picture? You reinforce the same kinds of points you have used before with the individual family members, but you're stressing the possibilities that the family can change and that the family can get well.

These are the tools you have to work with in handling objections and put-offs, and they will work for you if you are willing to try them. Obviously it's not all going to go like clockwork, but you might be surprised at how anxious family members are to try something new, and they might give you such agreements as,

"I'll go one time, and that's that!" or, "Well, if this will pacify you." That's fine! The idea is that you want to get this family of yours into some kind of help, ideally professional help with follow-up into self-help groups. So you catch the ball any way they'll throw it to you! After all, you're the one taking the major risk, and you're the one who will have the most to gain by beginning to deal openly with the family secret.

In the next chapter, you'll learn about getting started, and you will find that there will be continuing objections and put-offs in many stages of these processes from now on. You continue to handle them the same way. Offer alternative solutions so that there's really no way family members can weasel out of making some kind of commitment to at least *investigate* the potential for getting well!

8
Getting Started—
Here's How!

Now we come to the tough part. Assume that you have succeeded in persuading family members to agree to getting help in handling the family secret. You have been shopping for therapists, treatment centers, or self-help groups, and have selected one or more. The fateful day for the first session is upon you. Chances are, you keep wondering where all the butterflies are coming from. This may seem like it's much tougher than you had bargained for, but remember, the hardest part was getting people to agree, first of all, even to own up to the family secret. Working through identifying what the secret was, and then fixing the responsibility on the person to whom it belonged, was the hardest part.

Now you are ready to begin the healing process. You may want to make a previsit to the treatment center, program, or therapist before the family becomes involved. This also may be something that the therapist you've selected will ask you to do, just to get a handle on what the problem really is and not waste valuable therapy time in restating that for all to hear.

It's up to you to be the one to get started. If you have not had experience with therapy, don't worry. There's really nothing to be afraid of. The process of therapy is one of simply looking at alternatives for the ways in which we behave, finding new pathways to do things in a much healthier and, ideally, happier fashion than before. Of course, a lot of this depends on your attitude as you approach the process of getting well. You have to remember all along that this is something you *want* to do. It's not something that anyone is making you do, and it's certainly not a punishment for something that you have done in the past. It's rather a new step forward, one that you take with confidence.

Other members of the family will be just as anxious as you are. Whether they have had a good deal of therapy or none at all, going in together to talk about a problem will be a new experience. You still may be fighting objections along the way, such questions cropping up as, "Why do we need a stranger to be talking with us?"; "What do we hope to accomplish by all this anyhow?"; "Can we really *afford* this?" You need to be prepared to answer all of these questions.

Let's start with the last one. Your family cannot afford *not* to seek help with this problem any longer. And since you have many alternatives all the way from self-help groups, which don't cost anything, to treatment programs and individual therapy sessions, you can pretty much call your own shots regarding the cost of family treatment. Remember also that if you have insurance, most companies will pay a percentage of your treatment costs or a certain number of visits, depending upon your policy. So don't let cost keep you away from therapy. You can't really put a price on a family being well, but you can put a terrible price on a family that remains sick!

The question "Do we really need a stranger to be able to talk?" is a good one, and crops up more often than you would think. The answer is that the therapist only starts out being a stranger, but he or she ends up being an intimate member of the process for getting well. Notice I said "member of the process" as opposed to "member of the family." It's the therapist's responsibility to stand slightly outside the family picture and be able to look in, to help guide you and, in some cases, to give direct instructions to you, but in all cases to listen attentively in order to gain clues as to exactly how the family has been behaving in the past, how it is behaving now, and how best to help it change it's behavior in the future.

Not all the family members are going to like the therapist you have selected. Maybe none of them will. But therapy is not built around personality, and it will be up to you and the family to process each and every session when you are back home together. Process what you have learned, process what you did not learn, and process your feelings about even being in therapy. Most therapists are just as anxious to have feedback from you as you are to have feedback from them. They'll want to know how you're feeling about the work you are doing. So assure the family members before you get started that you will all have an opportunity to air your feelings after each session.

Some families have made it a point to go out to dinner together after their family sessions in therapy. They have found this is a good time to combine family time, a good meal, and a chance to discuss some of the things that went on in the family session. Other families find the pain too strong to be together in a public place and will separate and not get together for hours, but then will meet—usually at breakfast—and make it a point to discuss what happened in the session of the previous evening and how they want to respond to the information they received.

Some family members will have suddenly found themselves "unavoidably" detained from making the family sessions. This is not so much a slam at you as it is simple fear and an unwillingness to want to get involved in the therapy process in the first place. There is safety in numbers! Therefore, you need to go back to your tools about what has made it possible for the family member not to put a priority on the preset time that you had established for the therapy session or the group meeting. Younger members of the family, particularly teenagers, will tend to consider all of this as "a big waste of time." Regardless, it's up to you to be in control of the situation. If teenagers have suddenly gotten themselves involved in projects that would take them away from the family session time, you need to help them uninvolve themselves and stick to the game plan.

If you have to cajole family members in order to get started, do so! Tell them, "Come on, everyone, let's give this a chance. If we don't like it, we don't have to go back. And what we say is in confidence, so we don't have to worry about our secret being used to exploit us." The cajoling comes with you getting just this side of begging for everyone to keep their promises to you in order to have the session succeed.

Advance Preparation

It would also be helpful in getting started if every family member has had an opportunity to write down a few short thoughts about what the family secret has meant to them. This will be helpful for your therapist or, if you're going to be in a self-help group, just to remind each other how differently and yet how very much in the same way the family secret has affected all of you.

A very important part of this writing-down process is not to share it with other family members outside of the therapy or the self-help program. Part of the value of getting well is for other family members to hear for the very first time certain things that have affected the other members of the family's lives. Sometimes this can be a very powerful tool in helping the family realize how much the secret has been a protective one. Let me give you an example of the case of Little Joey.

Little Joey was the youngest member of a family of six children. I guess he had been called Little Joey from the time he was old enough to respond to human words, but he wasn't little in brainpower, only in stature, and was the obvious baby and favorite of the family.

The family was involved in the treatment of alcoholism for the father, but, at the time I first met them, the family had been unsuccessful in getting the father even to talk about his drinking. The mother of the family, who we'll call Martha, agreed that an intervention was necessary, that she was unable to cope anymore with the nightly drinking and then the denial on behalf of her husband. The children ranged in age from twenty-four years down to Little Joey, who was twelve. Two of the brothers were married, and their wives were going to participate in the intervention. The other children were an eighteen-year-old unmarried girl, a sixteen-year-old unmarried girl, a fourteen-year-old boy, and Little Joey.

In the initial stages of preparing for an intervention, I have each of the family members prepare their list of indictments, and also ask them to be thinking about a consequence that they will give to the person who is the subject of the intervention, in the event that the subject refuses to get help for the problem, and the consequence must be enacted. I'm very careful to ask each intervention participant not to share his or her list of indictments with one another, in order to preserve the shock value described earlier. At the assessment session, where all of the indictments were to be read, we did not make it totally around the circle, and most of the incidents that had been relayed by the other family members were the kinds of things I have come to expect over the years of being an interventionist and therapist particularly in chemical dependency. The mother (Martha) talked about her embarrassment at her husband's getting drunk at her office party and making lewd remarks and passes at some of her co-workers. I watched carefully, and there were almost no raised eyebrows among the children present, which told me that this was not a behavior they were unaware of. Some of the reaction of the children came to more specific cases when Martha related incidents that had occurred before they were really aware of the alcohol problem during the early marriage years.

One of the married sons talked about his disappointment in his father for not being able to participate in the family business.

Again, no surprise from anyone. The daughters-in-law both talked about their love for their father-in-law, but both also talked about being very uneasy and uncomfortable around him when he was drinking. Neither of them had much of conse- quence to present, but both daughters-in-law did have specific incidents in their indictments by date, name, and place (at their house) when they felt their father-in-law had been loud and boisterous and had been an embarrassment to them in front of their friends. One daughter-in-law used an incident of attending a football game with her father-in-law and wondering whether or not she could get him out of the stadium before he made "a total ass of himself." Pretty good indictment material. But we still had not heard from Little Joey.

At the next rehearsal session, the fourteen-year-old and six- teen-year-old children talked about trying very hard to please Dad and listed a couple of school functions and sports activities in which they had taken some teasing from their friends related to Dad's obvious drinking and not being quite in control of himself. Since some of the other family members had been involved in these incidents, there were still no surprises. I kept watching Little Joey as he folded and unfolded the piece of Big Chief tablet paper that he had been writing upon, apparently over several days.

At last it came time for Little Joey, and he announced first of all in the format of the intervention, "Daddy, I love you very much, and I want to help you." Little Joey then proceeded to lay on me what was something of a bombshell, because it had not come up before in any of the preparations or any of the precoun- seling work that I had done. Joey announced, "As I'm sure you know, I have a problem wetting the bed." He looked down at his paper, and the rest of the family members had a difficult time looking at him, since they all knew that this had been a problem with Little Joey for some time, and they had all been involved in the process of helping him break the bedwetting habit.

But now came the divulgence of the great secret that Little

Joey had been carrying around, a secret that nobody else in the family knew and one that became totally devastating to everyone. Little Joey began his story, reading from his paper.

"My best friend Tommy and I play together a lot after school," he said. "We always play with just each other because nobody else will play with us. Tommy has a problem, too. And since we are both 'outcasts' and 'freaks,' I'm sure glad I have Tommy as my friend." At this point, the family members were astounded, and so was I. There was nothing physically wrong with Little Joey. What had made him think that he was a freak? And yet here he was reading from his own paper his innermost thoughts. Some of the family members started to protest, and I motioned with my hand for them to keep quiet and let Joey proceed, which he did.

"Since Tommy and I both wet the bed, that makes us both freaks, and since we are both freaks, the other kids make fun of us. Tommy's daddy drinks too, and I guess that's what keeps us together. So I'm not sure, Dad, whether you should stop drinking or not. Because if you were to stop drinking, I might lose my one and only friend, Tommy."

Well! Do you believe there wasn't a dry eye left, including those of yours truly? This was a jolting, terrible revelation from a twelve-year-old boy who had been locked in a fear for so long, and the secret he had kept in him was a secret only from the other family members. This secret was that he considered himself a freak because of a problem with wetting the bed. And he was taking the biggest risk of his life in divulging this secret in front of his family. Yet he was faced with a problem that would keep his father from trying to get well and get help because it would cost Little Joey his best friend, or so he thought.

Here then was a double family secret that was coming to roost: the father's drinking problem and Joey's feelings about himself. The revelation had a tremendous impact because no one had read each other's indictment or consequence list. You can imagine that if they had all sat down and worked on them together and Little Joey had divulged his feelings in that manner, some other family members, including Mom, might not ever have let that come to the attention of the rest of the group. Joey's feelings might have been struck out and thus buried, and he never would have had a chance to express them.

Instead, as soon as Joey had folded away his paper, all of the rest of the family rushed to him and hugged him and showed more affection to him than he'd had in a long time. They all assured him that he was not a freak, and they all said things like, "I had no idea you felt like that," and, "Joey, you're a brave boy!" So we already had the makings for beginning a healing process as the family worked on the overall problem of an alcoholic husband and father.

That's why I'm suggesting that you prepare for your first sessions as I have outlined in this chapter, doing it individually and not sharing it. When you get into the family session and these thoughts are shared, sometimes their impact makes even the most borderline member of the family, who didn't really want to participate in this process, sit up and take notice and decide he or she needs to be a part of the healing process.

As you begin the family sessions, there will be some uneasiness, some anxiety that will be expressed, and some that will not be expressed. Leave the work of getting comfortable to the therapist who is conducting the session. If you're in a self-help group, the group members will make you feel welcome. You will know very quickly that you are not alone in this situation.

Getting Everybody There

It's important in the phase of getting started that you make sure everybody shows up when they're supposed to. Several times I have had family sessions fail to get going because transportation to my office was left up to other members, who "suddenly developed other problems" and never did show up! The clear solution is that as many family members as possible come in one car, or at least come in a caravan of one car following the other, so there's no chance of anybody ducking out.

Also, try to make a reward out of the whole situation. For example, it might be a good idea to plan on having a bite to eat together after the session, even before you learn about the business of processing what's happening in the sessions. If you don't want to go to that much trouble to have a full meal, maybe you could all at least go for an ice-cream cone or a frozen yogurt, or even just to have a Coke or a cup of coffee.

Let's look for a moment at the possibility that, even though all of the family members have agreed to come to a session, some of them do not show up for one reason or another. That should not deter you! You and whatever other family members are available need to get started. This is an interesting phenomenon that happens many, many times. People will come into therapy without the very person or persons who need to be there, but they continue to plug away, working at their own issues, and sooner or later the person or persons who needed to be there but have avoided it will find their way into treatment. This isn't always the case, but more times than not, I have had this work.

One woman, Sheila, was with a husband, Don, who was abusing marijuana and had begun to use cocaine and was obviously becoming addicted. He refused to come into treatment, refused even to do an assessment session around the problem, in spite of her threats to leave him or to have him move out of the house. She sat tearfully in my office, wringing her hands and asking what she should do. I asked Sheila to go ahead and start our significant-other or codependent program of treatment, and not to worry about him. She wondered how this would be of help to her. I asked her just to trust the process and to begin the treatment program as if her husband were in treatment with her, so she did.

Sheila would come to the education sessions. She was assigned an individual therapist and faithfully kept her meetings with that person. She also was installed as a member in a new codependent group and became very active in it week by week as she met at our treatment center. Still no sign of Don. At about week four or five, Sheila reported that her husband was beginning to wonder, "What do you do down there anyhow?" She would simply remark on the lectures that she had heard and what support she was getting from the group, finding out that she was not alone with this problem.

Eventually Don's curiosity got the better of him, and while he made no promises whatsoever even to stay with the program, he came in at Sheila's invitation just to hear one of the lectures. After hearing the lecture, Don asked to see my partner. (He was not anxious to see me at all, considering me the "bad guy" who was working with his wife.) This is typical, and we arranged for him to have a private session with my partner, Paul Staley.

After the session, Don agreed that he would come into treatment "just to see what it was all about." By the time everything was set up and he was ready to start, he found a way to go out of town and was absent for two weeks. So it was actually seven weeks into treatment before this husband ever joined his wife in coming into the program. But she had steadfastly remained working on getting herself well and finally was rewarded by her husband coming into treatment.

When he came in, Don was hostile and belligerent but determined that if it was something Sheila could do, he could do it also. The couple graduated our treatment program together with Don being drug-free and telling the story many times about how Sheila had been "the leader of the pack" that got him to finally come in and look at the issues!

So you see, her persistence had paid off. That's why I tell people to start treatment or start with a self-help group even if everyone else stands you up. They will come through eventually, even though it may seem dark, dismal, and lonely for you at the beginning.

Assigning Priority

Another important phase of getting started is the assignment of priority. It's pretty easy to give up, particularly if after the first session things have not gone very well and it's been a little scarier than you thought. So before you even get going in the process, all family members must agree that they will give therapy a fair shot. That means clearing other things from the schedule, as we've discussed before, and agreeing upon a specific period of time to participate in the examination process of therapy and treatment.

Self-help groups have no beginning and no end, so you can drop in or drop out of them anytime. I have found it to be more helpful if you can seek formalized treatment so that there can be a set time period, showing the family members they are not going to be locked in to a program forever, but that they will have to make a commitment for a certain number of weeks or months. Most therapists I know will not want to take on a family for treatment without a commitment of, say, three months. This means the family agrees to meet at least once a week for a period of three months.

At the end of the three-month period, the therapist and the family can evaluate the progress they have made. "Where do we go from here?" "What do you think we've accomplished?" "How do you all feel about going on for another three months?" These are all appropriate questions that will be asked at the conclusion of the first three-month period. Whether you decide to continue will depend on a number of factors, including whether or not you can continue to afford treatment and whether or not you really see progress.

If you will trust the process of therapy, you will be amazed at how much you accomplish and how differently you are acting with each other. It is this very interaction that is enabling you to drop the family secret and begin to deal with it openly as a means of getting well. Remember, the family secret has also been a means of keeping you together, and you may find that, once the family secret has been openly talked about in such an aggressive manner as family therapy, some family members are drifting away from the group as a whole. Don't be frightened by this. It's a natural element of getting well and something that probably should happen. Who in the world wants a family to stay together based on sickness? Not I! You want your family to stay together because it chooses to do so out of love, care, and concern for one another, not because it is the only means of survival.

Your patience is going to be tested in the process of getting started. More excuses for not going will crop up than you ever imagined. Strange "sicknesses" will develop almost overnight; the closet of anxieties will be wide open, and you can count on at least seven or eight different and apparently valid reasons why so-and-so will not be able to attend the first session. But you have to go right back to the tools, telling family members that you're going even if they don't go. You're using some element of shame here, but also asking them and pleading with them just to give it one shot.

If you can also trust the process, you will find that the family will more easily become hooked on the idea of treatment and will begin to feel rewards from the very first session. What are these rewards? The biggest reward will be that the family is able to sit down and talk together, and those that won't talk will be able to *listen* together. This is probably something that hasn't been done in your family for some time. That silence is one of the reasons the family secret has been allowed to flourish.

Good luck with the process of getting started! Don't back off your intentions to stay with it. It's going to be up to you to let the rest of the family understand that getting well can be fun!

9
Monitoring Results

As with every good project that is undertaken, you are anxious for results. There's nothing wrong with that! This chapter will provide some guidelines that will help you see what has been accomplished and what is still left to be done. To do that, start by taking your "emotional temperature." Do this by asking, "How is my life changing?"

The answer may startle you; maybe there's no *noticeable* change at all; maybe everything that is happening is subtle, much like a pastel drawing or a watercolor, in contrast to a boldly painted oil or acrylic canvas.

But you can count on one thing for sure: there *are* changes taking place! How can they be measured? Use the following questions as guidelines:

- "Do I find myself being more aggressive in my dealings with others, instead of always being on the defensive?"
- "Am I able to answer questions in a direct, concise fashion?"

- "Have I found myself talking a lot more about members of my family?"
- "Do I seem to want more social contacts than before?"
- "Have I found myself setting limits on the amount of help I offer to family members? Without feeling guilty?"

Answering these questions can help you take your emotional temperature. If you answered yes to some of these questions, you are breaking the shackles of the family secret. More "yes" answers are a measure of your continuing the get-well process.

As the family secret begins to be tackled, as family members seek treatment, then you begin a period of personal growth that has been stunted perhaps for many years. Let's look at each of these new tools in more detail.

Aggressiveness

Being more aggressive means that you are not afraid to let down your guard. You become more eager to assert yourself without leaving a possible escape route. Perhaps in the past, when people would talk or try to talk to you about your family, you would say things like, "Why do you ask that?" "Who told you about *that?*" and so forth.

Now, there is no need for you to be defensive. You can answer questions with some confidence, and you can counter with questions of your own, asking about *their* family, for instance. In other words, you no longer have to be so protective of your family members as you've probably been in the past.

You can be a little more aggressive by volunteering information about your family that you have not before. For example: "I talked to my sister in Boston yesterday, and she said to say 'Hi!' "

Before, you may have never volunteered any such information, but now you can drop the mantle of protection. Or you might say to a friend that you would be happy to meet him or her "after I drop some things off to Mom." In the past, your friend might never have heard you mention your mother, but would instead have been treated to something like: "Sorry, I can't meet you. I have *other* plans." Your friend, try as he or she might, could not get you to divulge that those "other" plans really involved your dropping by your terribly overweight and food-binging mother to make sure she wasn't once again just sitting in front of the TV, gorging herself!

Remember, it doesn't matter what the secret is in a family. To the family, it's all-consuming.

Directness

The second question measures your use of direct answers. You can hold your head up high and give straightforward answers to questions that express genuine concern. You no longer have to create complicated and tangled "webs to deceive," as before.

Using this tool will give you great relief. For example, your friend may have asked, "How's your sister in Boston? I never hear you talk of her anymore!" To which you can reply, "She's doing much better now that she has decided to seek marriage counseling; they're going to try again. By the way, she said to tell you, 'Hi!' "

Being able to give such an answer is a tremendous release from being secretive. That's why we are using it as a good tool for monitoring your getting better. Using this tool doesn't mean you suddenly have to turn into some kind of blabbermouth about every single thing each family member is doing, but it *does* mean that you can hold your head up and answer questions directly and concisely; you no longer have to protect the family member and the secret.

Proud Sharing

The third guideline for taking your emotional temperature is "proud sharing." Simply stated, this means that you are beginning to open up and tell people more about your family, the little accomplishments and maybe even some of the disappointments that have happened to them. But the big difference in *your* getting well is that you are doing some prideful—not shame-faced—sharing.

In the past, before the family began the get-well process, you would steer far clear of volunteering any of even the smallest accomplishments. You wanted to keep other folks as far away as possible from knowing anything about your family, good or bad, and you really had nowhere to go with nice little pieces of prideful sharing. Now you have! When you find yourself doing a little good old-fashioned boasting, then you are using the tool that is helping you monitor yourself; your emotional temperature is getting more stabilized all the time!

Social Contacts

Number four in your new tool list is establishing and maintaining social contacts. You are progressing if you are finding yourself seeking more contact with others, if you have begun to free yourself from being chained to the family. In other words it's beginning to be OK for you to finally leave home, so to speak.

Before, you may have made up excuses to *avoid* social contacts, things like dinner invitations that would have trapped you into possible conversations about your family. For you, these may have been very painful times, always caught up in lying, lying, and *more* lying in order to protect the family secret. But since you are giving up ownership of the family secret, it becomes OK for you to leave your cocoon and begin to test your new social wings!

You do not have to turn down any kind of invitation, because you can freely talk about your family in the secure knowledge that it's OK; people are anxious for successes in families, theirs *and* yours. The more you spend time with other people, going places and doing things, the more you will find that you can really dispose of most questions about family fairly quickly, directly, and on an upbeat scale, thus allowing you to move on to other topics. It's when you *avoided* social contact that other people began to press you for the whys and wherefores that made you prefer to hide in your own little closet instead of subject yourself to the outside world.

No more! Enough! You can pull out your dancing shoes or your golf clubs and tennis racket! Get back in the swimming pool! Haul out the old bicycle and the picnic basket! Start *living* again!

Setting Limits

The final sign of progress is setting limits. The more you learn to say no to family requests for help that really hasn't been helpful at all, the better you are at stabilizing yourself *and* them! I once treated a woman in her codependence to her alcoholic boyfriend. Vera entered treatment, but he refused. She had a responsible position in marketing; he was an unemployed construction worker without a car. He would ask her for her car so he could spend his days visiting friends who lived in the mountain towns surrounding the city.

Vera, good codependent that she was and fearful of losing this not very rewarding relationship, would loan him her car. Secretly, she was very angry that he would not be spending his time in her car looking for work, which he desperately needed. But Vera was protecting a family secret. All of her friends at work—and she had plenty because she was popular and outgoing—had been led to believe she was in a relationship with a very successful *contractor*, not just a framing carpenter who spent much time on the unemployment list, drinking and verbally abusing her.

When Vera began to get well and started shedding the secret about her boyfriend, she did so by refusing to "help" him anymore by giving him her car. She set a hard-and-fast rule. He could drop her off at her work, use the car to seek gainful employment, and then present her with some kind of proof that he had visited job sites or contractors to get work.

This may sound as if she was emasculating him, that she was treating him like a little kid, demanding a "note from the teacher." But what Vera was really doing was stopping the enabling patterns in which she had become trapped, shedding the secret by sharing with her closest friends what her life was *really* like, and thus throwing off a blanket of guilt that she had been wearing for the five years of their live-in relationship.

In short, Vera was setting limits, something she had been afraid of before, and something that her guarding of *her* family secret had nurtured. For Vera, entering treatment and beginning work on her codependency was the beginning of her taking a long look at the entire relationship and the ways in which her emotional temperature had climbed way out of sight.

Monitoring Your Family

So these five new tools can help in the monitoring process for how you're doing. Now, how about the rest of the family? How is the family changing, or how are they *resisting* change?

This part is pretty simple. You only have to observe whether family members are talking to one another in an openness that has not existed before. Has *glasnost* appeared in your family's world? If it's good enough for Soviet policy, why not let it work for you? Do you hear family members unplugging themselves from the rumor network and putting other family members in direct touch with each other? Are family members getting together more often than in the past? Do they seem to have stopped avoiding each other, or has it become even more difficult to get everyone together?

Not only can you make these observations, you can *confront* family members about their behavior. If family members are not going along with their wellness program, then you need to confront that. They are resisting change, and for you that's simply no longer acceptable.

Be in tune with whether family members are keeping their schedule for therapy or self-help group. When they start to break out of the structure, then they are *resisting* the changes. You will have to gain some courage to confront, but confront you must!

Consider yourself the driving force behind the whole project. Take all the opportunities that you can to reinforce successes by telling other family members how well *you* are doing. Keep them aware that the therapy process is providing a payoff for you, one that is measurable in terms of how much better you feel, act, and *are!*

As in all sickness, once the initial crisis is over, there is a tendency to slack off. The further you allow yourself or your family to get from the crisis without taking action, the less it seems necessary to take any further action! So, you need to use a tool of reminding the family how things were; don't let them get lazy in the get-well process.

Your monitoring of the results does two things. First, you get a pretty good readout on yourself, that is, how things seem to be changing for you. Second, you get a *very* good readout on who may be dragging their feet in the family's get-well process.

You can get a check on your own feelings by asking your therapist, your sponsor, or other group members, "How do I seem to be doing?" This is a tool that New York's mayor, Ed Koch, uses all the time. He goes through the streets working the crowd over and over with "How'm I doing?" Granted, he sometimes doesn't get the answer he's looking for, but it's a very good tool for his taking the emotional temperature of that great city!

You may not get the answers you wanted either, but take the risk and verify your feelings about yourself anyhow! Do the same thing with the other family members. Ask them, "Hey, gang! How does it feel for everyone right now? *I* feel great being with all of you tonight. How does everyone else feel?"

Perhaps you are thinking, "I could *never* say things like that! *My* family would hoot and jeer and laugh me right out of the house!"

Don't be so sure! Stranger things have happened; try taking

the risk, and find out for yourself! When I wrote my book *Loving an Alcoholic,* I specifically asked codependents to take risks and *try* the things I was suggesting, things that required much courage perhaps, but that were absolutely necessary if codependents' lives were going to get better in their relationship with an alcoholic. I continue to receive letters from all around the country from codependents—"significant others" as I called them in the book—who tell me of not wanting to try the new tools, but taking the risk and doing it, and how *glad* they were!

In my lectures on loving an alcoholic, I challenge the audience members to go ahead and just *try* the use of the tools. I ask them to see for themselves the results they can get. So I'm not going to let *you* off the hook with this one, either!

You've got to promise that you will at least break out of the mold you see for yourself and *risk* asking the kinds of questions of your family that I am suggesting. Sure, some family members will hurl insults at you about being the "family therapist" or calling you "Dr. Know-It-All," but as the saying goes, "no pain, no gain!"

You can handle it, and the results are going to be worth it! It's so important that you have a monitor on the results of breaking up the family secret so that it is stopped in its tracks. Isn't taking a little derision from other family members worth the ultimate payoff? If you aren't willing to monitor the results and to plug the leaking holes in the dam, then all your hard work will have been for naught.

Of course, these actions will be difficult. They're a change from the way things have been in the past. It's been that way, that *sick* way, for so long that it has come to seem normal for you and your family. Isn't that sad? The idea of this book is to help you see that things can be *different,* and by being different in the sense of dislodging the family secret, things can ultimately be better!

Monitor your own results by using the five-question list at the beginning of this chapter.

Monitor the rest of the family and try to pinpoint if and how the family is changing. Where you see resistance, confront it, and remind the family how it can be different and of the rewards that *you* are experiencing as a result of the work *you* are doing.

Most of all, don't be discouraged if the results are not as quick or as thorough as you had planned. You have spent a long time getting sick; you need to have some time to get well. Take the time! Do the hard work now!

10
Watching Out for Failure

"Whatever do we have now?" you may be asking yourself, almost in disbelief. "Can this be true? Has someone in our family thought up a *new* secret to replace the one we have?"

You might have to give yourself a reality check on this one! But don't worry, you're OK. It could *really* be happening. Someone in the family has begun the use of another family secret to accomplish one of two things: either the family member wants to replace the existing secret, or he or she wants to *cover* the old secret!

What would be the sense in that? As we have discussed before, your family may simply have a great *need* for one of these secrets, and someone—or maybe more than one person—is running scared. That person is seeing the possibility that this family will not have a secret in which to wallow anymore; there will be no "glue" to bind everyone together, and that means the family member believes the family *needs* something like a secret to keep everyone in touch!

Kind of sad, isn't it? The family operating in this manner has needed a secret to stay together, some "darkness" members can share about each other, some fact that, if leaked to the outside world, might destroy the family. As long as there can be a secret of one kind or another, then, some might feel, "We are going to have to stick together."

The preceding chapters have given you tools that will help you ferret out and destroy the power of the family secret. If you have succeeded, *this* is when someone will dig up a new secret that hasn't been dealt with. Or (and this is the really sad part) they will *create* a new secret!

It may be hard to believe, but just imagine to what lengths someone in *your* family might go if that person needed to create a new secret to divert attention from the one that you are working on!

Here's an example. Let us say the family secret for your group is a divorce, in a family where such an act has been unthinkable due, let's say, to strict religious mores. Just when everyone has stopped protecting the parties involved and has begun to see that this marital situation needs to be brought out of the anxiety closet, another family member gets really sick.

I'm talking about a physical illness. A family member who is afraid that the disclosure and dealing with the divorce might blow the family irreparably apart suddenly becomes ill. An accident occurs, or this family member discovers something about him- or herself from a visit to a doctor. It can be an ordinary problem or a complicated one; it doesn't matter. What counts is that the family member discloses the disease, the condition, the accident, the tests, the *whatever* about his or her condition, and then plunges in with the killer statement: "Please, *no one* (boss, boyfriend, co-workers, Mom, Dad, you name it) must know about this!"

Suddenly, all the attention that has been placed on the divorce is shifted.

"What's wrong with Penny?" asks your mother. "She's so mysterious about something!"

"Sis," you hear, "what the hell is *wrong* with Penny? She looks terrible!"

Well, you get the idea, don't you? This family is going to turn its attention pretty quickly away from the main family secret and be embroiled in a new one! And *you* are unwittingly going to make it happen! You are going to get so tired of fielding all these questions about Penny—perhaps you have become the switch-board operator mentioned before—that you won't feel like connecting family members directly together. Instead, you may start saying, "Now, please, Dad, *don't* tell Mom! Penny doesn't want to worry her, but . . . ."

And so forth. This crisis just starts perpetuating all the old behaviors again, and before you know it, the family has a new secret, one that is going to demand so much attention that even if the divorce proceeds, no one will have to spend much time dealing with it, because everyone is in the middle of the *new* secret; Penny has made everyone a coconspirator in the new secret.

What's important here is Penny's belief that she can prevent the family from being torn apart by the secret of the divorce by having everyone rally around her and her new problem that she is begging everyone not to talk about. Interestingly enough, if the accident or disease or illness that has befallen Penny is serious enough, it might have the power to totally *eclipse* the original family secret.

How? Well, let's suppose that the divorce that is going to take place is between your mother and father. Maybe there's even a small scandal connected with it, such as the involvement of another man or woman. Now, here comes Penny, fearful that when the secret gets blown totally out of the family and becomes "public property," it will destroy her sense of family. She can weather the idea of a possible divorce; what she can't handle is having everyone *know* about it!

Penny is trying to take the focus off, to cover the family secret by creating a new one. When your mom and dad finally are a party to Penny's mysterious illness, they may even halt divorce proceedings! For sure, they will rally the rest of the family around poor Penny, and everyone will be drawn tighter and tighter into the new secret.

Penny may never be able to say effectively *why* she needs her illness or accident to be a secret; it will be good enough that she has created a diversionary tactic that would be the envy of many military experts.

This is going to ultimately lead to the failure of the first secret. If the divorce has already started or finished, the other family members will cover it up and band together to rally around Penny and her new secret. This will help take the pain away from the now public secret of the divorce because, when outsiders question you or other family members, you can quickly divert their attention away from the divorce and hint of your worry over "Penny's problem." When pressed about the problem, you or other family members can keep Penny's secret and simply say, "I can't talk about it."

It doesn't really matter that Penny's problem doesn't have to be a secret at all. What matters is that the family *reacts* to that tactic! Even more frightening is the understanding that your family feels they need a secret to really function as a family.

So you have to be aware of the possibility of failure coming your way in the form of another secret that appears or is created to drain the impact of the first secret. You can find yourself caught in this web before you know it! This is when you may realize how badly your family needs secrets and rumors about each other to keep glued together. It will amaze you at first, but ultimately it will completely *anger* you.

Thus, failure is always beckoning because there is a real fear that the family will be left with no secret at all, and then what would happen? It's as if the family *needed* the secret or secrets to survive, and in a way it does! Family members are not able to maintain healthy enough interfamily relationships unless they *know* something about each other that no one else knows. So what do they do? They continue to perpetuate these secrets; they make up new ones; they replace ones that are being threatened with disclosure. They will do almost *anything* to guarantee failure of the secret's disclosure and the healthy recovery from that disclosure!

It doesn't seem possible, does it? You work toward getting rid of family secrets because they prevent families from getting from the hurting side of the ledger to the healing side, and yet family members create *new* secrets out of fear that there won't *be* a family if there are no secrets!

You need to be on the alert for failure by using the following tools:

- Watch out for family members who have suddenly lost interest in the family secret that you are working on.
- Watch out for family members who suddenly seem distant.
- Watch out for family members who start making alliances with family members they haven't been too tight with in the past.

Family members who lose interest in the discussion, or who work around the secret that is current, tend to be plotting a new secret to replace the drama of the current secret. Members who are distant from you are seeking time away from you because you are a *threat* due to your insistence on disclosing the family secret. In other words, you become the "enemy" trying to "break up the family."

Family members who suddenly seem to start forming new alliances with each other are gaining momentum for sabotage! They are using the disclosure of the family secret as a new bonding between them, and you are sitting off in the corner wondering about this strange new alliance.

Examine these clues, and know that they are foretelling failure. You have to be on guard.

Don't be afraid to confront family members who are setting you up to fail. You have learned how to confront in this book. Ask questions like these:

- "It seems as if you are avoiding me lately. What's that all about?"
- "Is it possible that our getting rid of this damn secret is *scary* to you?"
- "What's making it hard for you to let go of this secret?"
- "It looks to me as if we *need* this secret to be a family . . . do you agree?"

Remember that letting go of the family secret is a lot like letting go of a lifeline. If you consider that the family secret might really *have* been the glue that has kept you together, then it makes sense that letting go might be plenty scary—not only for you but for the principal(s) involved, as well as the other family members.

When you sense failure is setting in, point out to other family members that you are just as frightened about letting go of this "monster" as they are. Keep focused on the *solutions* to the problems and not on the problems themselves. Say things of a supportive nature again, even though you have said them over and over:

- "I'm really excited about our family therapy!"
- "I feel change is becoming an important part of my life!"
- "It's great to see all of us getting well together!"

You may think there is no way that you could beat that kind of drum. But try it! You've got to pull out all the stops when you are trying to break up this sickness of the family secrets. For whatever flak you might receive, if you stick with the process, you can turn the possibility of failure into success.

Keep focused on the *solutions*. Ask yourself and other family members, "What do we have to do to make things *better?*"; "What do you need from *me* to help you make this work?"; "What do we need to do to move forward?"

In the following chapter, we'll continue with some of these ideas as we look at that menace that may be lurking in your family: the family saboteur!

11
The Family Saboteurs

It's almost inconceivable to realize that one or maybe more than one person in your family doesn't want the family to get well. "How can this possibly be?" you may lament. "I thought that everyone would want to stop all the nonsense that has been going on in our family and face the secrets that have been keeping us in this state of sickness for much too long!"

Wrong! There usually *is* someone who doesn't want it to work. You will have to determine who the family saboteur is, but you can count on the fact that there very probably is one. The saboteur is the person or persons in your family who feel threatened in giving up the protection of the family secret.

For the most part, these people really fear losing their family job, that is, the role they have assumed in being the family caretakers. It's like a nurse who has been doing private-duty nursing for a patient and then is no longer needed. She or he may go through a brief depression caused by losing a patient—the very thing the nurse is dedicated to.

In your family, getting well means losing the patient! At least that's what it means for the saboteur(s). Here's an example of a "significant other" who sabotaged her husband's treatment.

Jill had two young children, ages eight and eleven, and a cocaine-prone husband. Their lives were, of course, rapidly falling apart from the financial drain that resulted as husband Mark accelerated his drug habit. They were falling behind in all their monthly payments, since Mark was putting most of the payment money up his nose.

When they came to treatment, Jill had taken over managing the entire family. Mark was falling further and further out of touch with his children, growing further and further from his attractive wife of fourteen years. Jill had issued an ultimatum that is most common in these cases: "Either we get some help, or I'm taking the children and leaving this marriage!" she told him.

Mark confirmed that was the principal reason he was willing to enter our six-month program at Gateway Treatment Center; he didn't want to lose his children. It's very interesting that many men will feel they can afford the loss of a *wife*, but it's the emotional pull of the children they use as a primary reason for entering treatment.

At any rate, Mark, Jill, and their children started the long road to recovery. For weeks, the change was evident; Jill was brimming with happiness when we would see her at the center. She kept her individual therapy appointments with the therapist who was seeing her; she and Mark were prompt and appeared motivated at the lecture series, and both were active participants in their separate small-group therapies, which are an integral part of our program.

The children participated with gusto in the ten-week-long program that is run in conjunction with the parents' program, and I began to see a lot of evidence of Mark and Jill growing closer together. Each week, Mark was getting stronger; he was remaining drug-free and had found at least a temporary but effective way out of their financial dilemma. Mark had shared his addiction with his boss, and because Mark was a very valuable member of the law firm that employed him, the firm made a sizable loan to Mark at low interest rates, which bailed him out of his difficulties.

All this time, we could see that some changes were developing in the family. Mark and his children were becoming closer; it was, as a matter of fact, Mark who started bringing the kids to their group therapy. This was causing him to leave his downtown practice early one evening a week, but he seemed to be genuinely interested in the progress that the children were making, along with his and Jill's progress.

And then it happened. It was not quite as noticeable at first, but the pattern began to develop much more rapidly than usual. Jill started breaking her appointments for her individual sessions. Calls from her therapist were either unanswered or met with lame excuses as to why she had been unable to attend her important sessions.

Jill missed her small group once, then twice in a row, even though Mark was punctual and as enthusiastic as ever. When confronted about Jill's absence, Mark would simply say, "She's not feeling well."

When Jill failed to show for the third consecutive week, either for the lecture, individual therapy, or her small group, it was evident to all of us that Jill was evading and getting ready to leave the treatment program. When Mark simply dropped the kids off for their group and failed to come in himself as he always did, we knew that there was trouble brewing!

A phone call to Jill started a "mini-intervention" on her to get her back to the center.

"Jill," I said, "please just come in and talk to me. Tell me what's going on with you! We are all concerned about you and want to help. I promise you, if you still want to quit after we visit, then no one will stand in your way."

Jill *did* come in. She would not talk to her own therapist, but agreed to see me, since I had been the one who originally enrolled them in the treatment program. She was definitely prepared to quit treatment, and I suspected that Jill was preparing to sabotage the entire family's remaining in treatment.

Jill told me that things were indeed getting better at home. She and Mark were communicating more; their sex life had resumed after a long absence, and they were definitely pulling out of their financial problems.

"Then what's making you want to quit?" I asked.

"I just don't think I *need* it anymore," Jill replied.

This is always a clue for me that someone has a hidden agenda for the real reason they want to quit. I encouraged Jill to tell me what things were *really* like at home, now that Mark was in treatment and had not used cocaine for several weeks. She informed me that the biggest change was Mark's taking responsibility again, and that she could see a really positive change in the relationship between Mark and their children.

"Tell me about that," I insisted.

"Well," Jill started, getting teary as she began, "for example, when Mark comes home—the minute he hits the front door, actually—the kids can't *wait* to throw themselves at him!"

Aha! The saboteur was about to be unmasked!

"What makes that so different?" I asked.

"Well, for months and months, while Mark was half wiped out with coke, the kids didn't give a damn if he was home or not! *I* was the one who listened to their school tales, and gave them encouragement in their sports and scouts ... now it's *Mark* who's important to them!"

Jill was crying unabashedly.

"It sounds as if that's painful for you ... as if maybe you're not *needed* anymore?" I threw out the grabber line to her. She bit, hard, and my saboteur was nailed!

"Hell, no!" Jill fairly came out of her chair. *"No one* needs me anymore!"

For Jill, you see, the prospect of her family's getting well meant that she was not going to be needed anymore, and it was just too painful for her to contemplate. So she stopped coming to treatment. She would have even embarked on a full-scale effort to drop *everyone* from treatment, so that she could return to the role she had been filling for such a long time, that of the primary care giver! Jill was willing to sabotage herself and the rest of the gang just for that very basic human emotion, the desire to be needed!

Fortunately, Jill responded to the confrontation about what she was doing, and she clearly saw that she was poised on the brink of allowing Mark to quit treatment and even go back to using cocaine socially (as long as it didn't get "out of hand"), in order to protect her turf!

"It was crazy!" she shared with her group after returning to the program. "I was actually going to settle for Mark's using coke again, just so I could get my needs met! I thought my kids, particularly, didn't need me anymore, and I just couldn't let that happen!"

This episode points out another important trap to be aware of. Mark was the toughest guy to convince about his wife's sabotage attempt! He could not conceive that she would be willing to forgo treatment, remove the threat of separation and divorce, and go back to how it was, just because she was feeling unneeded.

You, too, will find it hard to think that someone, particularly a member of your own family, could want to sabotage treatment and wellness.

To avoid that trap, you must put *everyone* on your "suspect" list! In other words, everyone is capable of playing the saboteur, when push comes to shove! When a family member is feeling threatened by the recovery process, then he or she reverts to the primary instincts that we all have: take care of number one first!

You will find twin brothers or sisters subverting the get-well process. Mothers and fathers, grandparents, and even your own children are quite willing to jump into the dark cloak of the saboteur, if it will protect their "turf."

Locating the saboteur becomes a matter of your finest detective work, with a little help from some tools I'll give you.

"Elementary, my dear Watson!" you may echo the famous

Sherlock Holmes in your eagerness to ferret out the culprit in your family. And in a way, it *is* elementary. Here's what to look for and the tools that you can use to do it.

First and foremost, decide who has the most to lose by the family continuing to get well. Remember, this person is not necessarily the holder of the family secret, but someone else who has been filling a big role that may no longer be necessary when the family starts on the path to wellness.

Second, observe which family member is beginning to carp at what's happening in the therapy groups or self-help programs in which your family is involved. Is he or she starting to complain that "nothing's getting done" or that "this (bleep) is a waste of time!"? The saboteur is beginning to get fearful that he or she will be eliminated from the family picture if the family's secret is brought out, worked on, and banished!

People within a family often want to stay sick, and thus keep everyone else sick too, just so they can continue to occupy their place of importance in the family. Most often this will be the role of caretaker; frequently the family member who is doing the sabotaging for treatment is the one who has the most responsibility for the family, responsibility that could well be shared or even abolished if other family members start to get well and assume their rightful roles on the responsibility ladder themselves!

Remember that the saboteur has been *handed* this role and has built it from a small bit part into a major speaking role, one that assures his or her "stardom" within the family as possibly the superhero in addition to being the primary caretaker.

No one who has had the starring role will be content to go back to being the understudy, so sabotage will be one method that will be employed to keep the family just the way it is.

The family saboteur was handed the role when he or she saw the need for it and jumped in to fill it, probably years ago. If the family secret revolves around your kid sister getting pregnant out of wedlock, this saboteur may have jumped in and adopted this baby as her own, raising the child with her own name, just to "protect" her sister. She became the family superheroine by stepping in, sacrificing herself, and *rescuing* not only her sister, but the rest of the family, from the "scandal" that was sure to leak out.

Now, with the family in treatment trying to unload this burden, the saboteur might lose her status within the family as "rescuer" and "superheroine." Just look at the terrible act of attempted assassination on President Ronald Reagan that young John Hinkley performed in order to get the *attention* of actress Jodie Foster. Or the esteem that Lynnette "Squeaky" Fromme felt surely would be hers in the Charles Manson "family" if she successfully killed President Gerald Ford.

Self-esteem is a hard-fought battle for many people, and no matter how it is achieved, it is difficult to give up. Remember that when you are taking a look at identifying the saboteur in your family.

As mentioned earlier, another big clue is a family member who starts making excuses for not attending whatever help source you are employing. Continued absences can spell the message out for you loud and clear: *someone* wants this project to fail!

The best way for you to confront this behavior is to do it directly. "It seems to me that you are missing a lot of our sessions," you might say. "What's the reason for that?"

You will probably get a lot of legitimate-sounding excuses, but be tuned in to the fact that you may be in the process of unmasking the saboteur. If you do, then confront the sabotage by pointing out how important it is for the family as a whole unit to have the opportunity to get well. Don't ever *guarantee* that the family is going to get better; it's the *process* of getting rid of the family secrets that is important.

Point out to the saboteur that he or she is in danger of sabotaging everyone else's chances to get well, even if he or she is not interested in getting well along with the rest of you.

Appeal to the saboteur's sense of pride: "My God, haven't we

all gone through this thing long enough? Isn't it time we had a
chance to get rid of this 'spooky secret' that's been around for so
long?"

Be prepared for the saboteur to turn on you! He or she doesn't
want you interfering with the possible loss of his or her position
in the family. The saboteur is going to start questioning *you*
about who put you in charge of the family, and the old stuff
about it "just being you who's so riled up" about the family.

You'll probably have to go ahead and take this blow to the
chin, but point out to the saboteur all the times when the secret
has backfired to the detriment of the family. These times will be
the initial reasons that you used in the first place to get the
family into acknowledging the secret and being willing to seek
help for it.

Urge the saboteur to at least give the rest of you a chance to
get well, even if he or she doesn't want to come along. That'll get
'em! Most family members who fear losing a caretaker job or
being a superhero can't stand the thought of being left out of
anything.

The saboteur may employ another method to do the dirty
work. This will be the "getting sick" routine, as described in the
preceding chapter. This approach can be very subtle, but it can
happen, so be on the lookout for it!

Related to this is the most insidious and potentially damaging
trick of the family saboteur. Your "Mata Hari" might just come
up with *another* secret to cover or replace the original one! The
new secret diverts attention away from the situation that is more
threatening to the saboteur.

Look at the example of a homosexual man or woman in your
family who is terribly fearful of continuing the secret-uncovering
process, because he or she is certain it will somehow lead to the
unmasking of the secret of his or her sexual orientation. To do so
would spell the end of his or her secretive lifestyle.

This person could start heavy drinking, even though not
alcoholic, simply to throw the trail cold on the other secret.

Painful as it may sound, sometimes this works, and the family begins to rally around the new flag of trouble, totally abandoning the real issue.

The clue for you is to observe sudden changes in behavior from a particular family member. Changes can be your warning sign that you may have stumbled onto your family saboteur.

These machinations don't have to be as severe or as dramatic for them to be effective as sabotage. Take the simple example of a schoolgirl who suddenly starts doing poor schoolwork, dropping dramatically in her grades just weeks before the family is scheduled to move to another part of town and hence another school district.

The girl creates first of all a crisis, in the matter of the dropping grades, and then she creates a secret by telling someone that she hates the place to which they are moving. Perhaps she doesn't hate the new location at all; what she hates is the idea of leaving a ready source of marijuana that is based in her present school.

That secret she simply can't divulge, so she creates a new secret of how she hates the new home, gets her closest friend to swear she won't tell her parents how she feels, and then proceeds to let her grades fall in order to force her parents to think again about moving to the new school district!

The young woman will protect her marijuana secret by finally "divulging" her "hate" for the new move, saying she has "kept this hate inside her" all this time, effectively forcing Mom and Dad and everyone else to consider giving up the move in order to help her get her "scholarship grades" back! She has created a secret in the "hate," thus covering her real secret, which is the marijuana use.

This actually happened; the young woman successfully thwarted the family move by creating this false hate secret. The problem for her should be obvious; her pot use increased even with the family putting off their projected move, and her grades went to hell anyhow! The *real* secret emerged in treatment, and now the girl is again getting the kinds of grades she needs for her college scholarship; she is free of drugs and has not created any more "secrets" to throw the bloodhounds off the trail!

So the saboteur can lurk anywhere in the family system. You have to be always on the lookout for him or her to leave you the clues that will entrap. One other little warning: Make certain that *you* don't become the saboteur! Stay tuned to treatment, and it won't happen!

12
The Payoffs for Getting Well

There *is* a reward for all this hard work, all this pain that has been surging to the surface because of your decision to end the family secret. The reward is really divided into three categories of payoff: (1) for you, (2) for the family, and (3) for the future generations.

The following description of these payoffs should help you identify them. It's important to identify the payoffs. Many times a reward or payoff happens, and it just sort of slides by unnoticed and, thus, unappreciated. Instead, you should have the full satisfaction of knowing that there has been a pot of gold at the end of the rainbow for you.

First let's look at just *you*. The payoffs for you are many, but chief among them is the release from the responsibility and fear that have been enslaving you ever since you learned of the family secret. You have been taking this responsibility, and it has been quite a burden; as you know, you can get rid of it by using the tools discussed throughout this book.

So the first reward is that you can be free of owning the

responsibility for the rest of the family. In other words, it's going to feel *very* good for you not to have to cover up anymore, for you to just let the chips fall where they may.

You have to continue to have courage; no matter what happens, the family secret—once out and being dealt with— begins to lose its power over you and the family. Think of the family secret as some kind of voracious dragon, and you are the St. George who is going to slay that dragon!

Knowing that you don't have to cover for anyone anymore should be quite a reward for you! If you were to think of all the energy that you have expended just to make up stories and keep the covert action going for your family, it would make you physically tired!

All that can be behind you. I have worked with many patients who have let out great sighs of relief in my office when they cast off this yoke of responsibility.

"Why didn't I do this before?" is the most common question.

"Because *fear* had you caught in its sticky, silken web," I am quick to reply. Once you have conquered fear by taking action toward ending the protection of the family secret, then the rest becomes easy.

So another reward for you is the loss of fear. You have finally decided that *nothing* can hurt you as much as the family secret was hurting you. It's similar to deciding that pricking your finger occasionally is much better than pounding your fingers with a heavy hammer! You are choosing to eliminate *pain* in your life by getting rid of your part of the family secret.

I worked not long ago with a difficult family situation, one in which the family secret was such a culprit that it was very hard even to identify it for a long time. Briefly, what happened was this: an attractive couple was seeing me about relationship problems that had occurred as a result of the wife being alcoholic. The wife, Doreen, was a very attractive, petite blond, the mother of two children.

This was the only marriage for Doreen and Rick, and he had

presented himself as the very loving and *very* patient spouse of an alcoholic. After they had been in treatment for awhile, I kept wondering why *I* was doing all the work in our sessions. Then the family secret was blurted out.

Rick was Jewish; no problem, no issue. Everyone knew it, and it was a very open part of his and Doreen's life. Doreen was very active in Jewish women's groups and was even going back to their synagogue to brush up on her Hebrew, something that was not going to be an easy task for her but was highly thought of by Rick and Rick's family. So what was the big secret?

Doreen wasn't Jewish at all; she never *had* been! She had pulled a sort of reverse passing situation, and had "become" Jewish early into her relationship with Rick, so that his family would approve! Rick had no idea. Doreen had started this covert action from the second date, when she had decided that marriage with Rick was what she wanted. His position, family, and eventual wealth were big factors.

As Doreen's drinking became more and more of an issue, that was the only thing that Doreen, Rick, and both of their families focused on. Doreen's mother was deceased, and her father lived in another state. Doreen and her father loved each other with that special father-daughter relationship that was enhanced after the death of Doreen's mother.

Her father knew of Doreen's plans to pass herself off as Jewish. She had the guts to do it and enlisted her father's aid to keep the secret, even from Rick. No wonder she had worked extra hard at the synagogue and had taken so much effort to learn Hebrew! Their rabbi had commented many times on Doreen's skill, never dreaming that she had never, *ever* been exposed to the beautiful but difficult language before.

It was in the middle of a particularly difficult marital session that Doreen blurted out the secret. At first, Rick was utterly devastated by the news.

"What will my parents think?" he said, nearly in tears. "My mother will *kill* me!" he whined.

It was evident where the power in this family reposed: in Rick's mother. She controlled everything that the young couple had done, from buying them their first furniture to carrying back the mortgage on a house that they really couldn't afford in the first place.

I could see that it was *Rick* who was going to try to keep on with the family secret, to protect his and Doreen's future. But in the course of therapy, they agreed that Doreen needed to come forth on her own and fess up. The decision was extremely traumatic, and Rick was convinced it would be the end for them as a family.

"My father will disown me. I will lose my interest in the family business!" he told me. This was the one thing that the family had always insisted on among their other children—that they remain married within their faith, assuring that children and grandchildren would carry on in that faith.

As it was, Doreen had been extremely faithful in raising and educating their two youngsters in the Jewish faith, so no one could fault her there. Rick, trembling nevertheless, stood by his wife as she braved her way into his family's living room and disclosed her secret.

Rick suddenly realized that he could be free of responsibility for trying to make things work between his mother and his wife, something that had been a constant source of irritation during their marriage, mostly because the mother was such a domineering person.

Doreen, for her part, knew now that part of the reason for her alcoholic drinking patterns was her effort to keep this secret buried within her, knowing that only one other person, her father, knew. The pressure grew and grew for Doreen, and her drinking escalated. But Rick had the first payoff.

As promised, his father was shocked, dismayed, and somewhat threatening. But Rick stood his ground. "This is something that you and Doreen will have to work on together," he told his father. "I love her and will not abandon her. She has raised

David and Ruthie in the faith; I can't ask for more."

Rick got a second payoff. He realized that he had lived in fear of his mother over many things, and Doreen's disclosure of her secret—which of course quickly became the *family* secret—gave Rick the courage to set many things straight with his mother.

Together, Doreen and Rick began to disclose her feat of learning Hebrew and practicing the faith even though she was Gentile. Their many friends were shocked, yet supportive and delighted that Rick and Doreen were sharing with them. Instead of driving people away, Rick and Doreen became the toast of their group of friends. No one, not one individual or couple, abandoned them!

The payoff for the family was that Rick and Doreen, refusing to keep the secret any longer, blew the cover for Rick's mother and father, and *they* had to get rid of the family secret. Together, Doreen and Rick's mother began to work out their differences, and Doreen's true personality began to shine through.

Her rewards were obvious, too. She no longer used this secret as the main reason for her drinking. Her denial vanished, and she began to get well. Rick continued to be amazed at his wife, developing a new pride in her and a deeper love.

This I share with you because it was a real stunner for me, too! I knew that something was lying underneath all the family troubles that were emerging, but I had been unable to tap into it. The release of this lovely couple and their parents from the "terrible secret," as Rick's mother called it, was wonderful. There were payoffs all around!

For Rick and Doreen's children, the future rewards should be obvious. They can have a great pride in their mother, who has so far raised them perhaps in a stronger faith than if she had been born Jewish. The children will not have the burden of keeping this secret, and they can be a source of strength for Doreen throughout a lifetime of recovery.

Think of the family secret as being a big pile of rubble that has blocked a major highway. Wellness, with the ending of any family secret, is the bulldozer that clears away that rubble!

There are other payoffs for the family that kicks the family secret. One of the biggest is a new and strong sense of honesty that suddenly must be established between family members. When a family secret is presented, many family members are tied together by it; they spend most or all of their time together either discussing and dissecting the family secret or adding to its power by enhancing some new pieces of information that make this thing bigger than life.

With the end of the family secret, family members have to reassess their relationships with each other. Here are some questions that all family members should ask:

- "What is my *real* place in this family?"
- "What is my relationship to others *without* the secret?"
- "What *other* things do I have in common with _____?"
- "Has my relationship with _____ been based solely on knowledge of the family secret?"
- "What is my new role in the family? What do I *want* it to be?"

You may think that the first and last questions are the same, but they are not. The first question asks where in the family structure you have been put. A certain pecking order has been assigned to you. Are you comfortable with that, or should you demand a different place in the family? What can you do to change that pecking order for everyone's benefit?

The last question asks about your *role.* Maybe you have been the chief enabler in the family, assuming all the responsibility for other family members. Do you want to continue that? If you had your "druthers," as my grandmother used to say, is that what you'd rather do from here on in? Or do you want to assume a *new* role? Your evaluation of the situation will tell you where you best fit in, and then it's up to you to carve out that role for yourself.

The honesty will be painful. You may suddenly realize that

you have absolutely nothing in common with a particular family member, now that the family secret is gone. In other words, all that was keeping you involved with this person was the shared knowledge of the secret; now that it is gone, you are faced with a lot of empty space between you!

What you then evaluate is what you can or *want* to do to replace that empty space with meaningful relationship material between you and the family member. It's not going to be easy, because you may come to the honest evaluation that there's not much of a payoff even if things work out between you; too much water may have passed under the bridge between you. If that happens, then just look at what you can do to build a *new* bridge, one plank at a time, to connect yourself with the family member.

This will require your skills and use of tools, starting with the honest and open discussion between the two of you about owning the fact that "we really haven't had much in common!" This should be followed by your question, "So what do we want to *do* about it?" *That's* the kind of wellness you should be practicing. While you may experience a new kind of pain from honestly evaluating your relationships with other members of your family, the new relationship that emerges from all of this effort will be stronger, healthier, and longer lasting than ever before.

There are other payoffs in this process. You will discover that your own self-esteem is on the rise. You will find a new energy in dealing with many things that you have put off for quite a while. Just think of all the projects that you put on hold because "this isn't the right time!" Well, now you have no excuses! You can and should get busy on the things you have been putting off in order to deal with the family secret. It may sound untrue, but believe me, you just can't *imagine* the amount of energy you have been consuming in keeping the family secret! If you want to test this, just ask yourself how many conversations you have had with any member of your family that *didn't* revolve around the family secret. These conversations might have even included the member who *was* the secret.

If you would redirect all that energy into more creative channels for yourself, you could accomplish wonders! Maybe you were always going to plan that special trip but "just couldn't" because "we can't leave now with [secret] going on!" Well, now you have no excuse. Or perhaps you've felt held back from taking that new job. Now what's stopping you?

It may be a little hard for you to realize that you can't use the family secret as an excuse any longer. It's important that you be willing to see the payoffs and go after them. Your family will reap the benefits in the long run, because they will be able to openly discuss how they have been trapped by the secret and now can discuss things among themselves more productively.

One of the great joys in our practice at Gateway is to see husbands and wives, fathers and sons, mothers and daughters, *talking* together about how they were covering the family secret and how relieved and free they now feel to get on with their lives!

It isn't going to happen overnight, but it will happen. If you are a runner or a bicycle racer, the sight of that finish line up ahead can spur you on to even greater bursts of energy, energy that you honestly believed was gone. It's the same with this business of family secrets; the payoff that you can see resulting from all the hard work that you are expending should urge you on into the final stretches. Be careful that you don't slip back into the old ways. It will be tempting to do this, because the old ways have been easier to handle for everyone. The new way of wellness is harder, but the rewards are infinitely greater!

Finally, keep reminding yourself that there *is* a pot of gold at the end of this rainbow. You *are* going to find a payoff, and you *are* going to make payoffs for yourself and others if they want them! If the alcoholic finds no joy in being sober, he or she is probably going to return to drink, no matter how good that person's intentions not to do so. The reason is that no payoff has been concocted for him or her; the person has made little or no effort to find the payoff of having alcohol out of his or her life.

When I wrote *The Joy of Being Sober*, it was with the prime intention of helping others find their own joy, their own payoff for sobriety. From the response from readers over the years, I know they have received the message loud and clear!

That's what I want for you in the realm of the family secret. Look for the payoffs that lie just down the road; don't give up the struggle now that you are this close to victory!

13
Erasing the Stigma

Face it, there might be a penalty for letting your secret out of the closet. Once the family secret has become generally known, you may start to feel some real paranoia about how you are being treated by friends, peers, or co-workers. Even the neighbors may seem to be treating you differently. In fact, they may really be acting differently toward you, or you may just be imagining it.

Nevertheless, there *will* be a subtle and maybe not so subtle change in the manner in which people will treat you, once you have gone public with the family secret. I think of the patient who was a government official and who was a dual abuser; that is, he had both an alcohol and a marijuana problem, quite severe.

When Tony entered treatment, he felt as if his substance abuse was simply a "weakness" that he could not control; his alcoholic heritage from a father and grandfather didn't matter to him. He was convinced that he was the beneficiary of a "character flaw" and, hence, would not share his treatment program with anyone.

However, eight or nine months later, after his six-month formal treatment program and with some solid AA and Narc-Anon experience, Tony was readily admitting to almost *anyone* that he was a recovering abuser; he was proud of it! It cost Tony some embarrassing moments, however, because not everyone wanted to be associated with him in recovery. It's funny; people who had no problem at all being seen with Tony when they were both getting sloshed at the favorite watering hole didn't bother to call during his recovery. It seems that when Tony got his sobriety and began *practicing* it and discussing his recovery, then there was some sort of stigma attached to him!

That's the thing to watch for. Some sort of backlash might come your way after the disclosure of the family secret. The reason is that people who hear of you getting well by dealing with and disposing of the family secret(s) are *threatened*. They have family secrets of their own but have probably done nothing at all about them, so you represent some sort of terrible threat! Sounds funny, doesn't it? Here you are taking a lot of risks in the get-well process, and you end up feeling distant from people who have been close to you, all because you have done something about your family secret, and *they* haven't!

The way for you to handle these situations is to dwell on the positive side of what disclosure and treatment have meant for you and the family. You will have to take the first steps to fend off the ice that may be forming, let's say, with close friends. As with so many other tools in this book, you must now take the initiative: "You know, Kate, I feel as if you are being distant with me lately. What's that all about?"

Here, you are invoking a good old standby tool, the "I feel" statement. When you begin confrontation of another person by the "I feel" method, you are asking *them* for help with *your* feelings, instead of confronting them about how *they* may feel. It works wonderfully. There is no reason for the other person to become defensive, because you are not saying, "Hey, Kate, why the hell are you treating me this way?"

If Kate denies that she is treating you any differently, then you can enlarge on your feelings by giving a specific clue: "Ever since I told you about the alcoholism in my family, I feel that you are putting up a wall between us. What's that all about?"

A likely explanation is that Kate is putting up a wall around *your* family alcoholism problem because she's got one of her own. So in Kate's eyes, there is a certain "stigma" now attached to you, and you need to break it down.

You do this not by confronting Kate that you know *she* has the same family problem, but rather by your positive endorsement of how different things are for you since your family got help with this family secret. Start with what's making you feel more sensitive: "You know, Kate, one of the things we have all been aware of since we started getting help for [Mom's] drinking is that we are really in tune with other people's feelings. I guess that's why I sense there is some sort of wall between us."

You are encouraging Kate to come out in the open and at least acknowledge that she feels differently about you and your family since knowing this secret. However, the real payoff is that Kate gets a sense of your finer-tuned awareness of feelings, and she will want to be a part of that process. Even if she doesn't rise to the occasion, you can keep on adding fuel to the fire of the get-well process by saying, "You know, Kate, it's so good to have friends like you who understand how hard it's been to hide this secret from the world for so long!"

Now, of course, you are playing directly into Kate's important role in your life, something that she will find hard to resist. Kate may continue to insist that nothing is wrong by saying, "Why do you feel that way?"

That's a perfect opening for you *not* to get defensive, but to tell her about specific instances when, once again, you have felt that Kate was distancing herself from you, as in, "When I talked about Mom eating so much better, you changed the subject to the theater subscription series." And then you plunge on: "I felt as if you were uncomfortable with me talking about Mom. Is that true, Kate?"

Now you are giving your friend Kate a perfect opportunity to say something like, "Well, yes, Ginny, I *am* uncomfortable but only [here Kate decides to go for it] because I never knew about your Mom's drinking, and I thought I was your best friend!"

Well, that's *one* scenario that could happen. Believe me, it *has* happened that way more than once. A direct assault on a person's supposed friendship by the stronger element of a family protecting its secret! You can counter this with the "Kates" by saying, "God, Kate, *nobody* knew! We kept it hidden in the darkest, most crowded closet we could find! To tell you would have been too big a risk for me. You see, I didn't want to risk losing your friendship if you found out. I certainly don't want to lose that friendship now because you know!"

Now you are giving Kate an opportunity to reaffirm her friendship with and for you, and also possibly to say, "Ginny, I've got a similar problem with my sister. I haven't known how to tell *you*, either!"

Now, in case you think that's just some cheap soap opera dialogue I have given you, rest assured it is almost verbatim from a case I worked with among two very close friends.

"How," you may ask, "if they were *really* close friends, could they *not* know about those kinds of problems?"

Good question, and my only answer is to refer you to the old adage, "Blood is thicker than water." Family secrets can be so powerful that even best friends will not be told, for fear the family will somehow be blackened beyond all repair—the stigma so great and the ultimate loss of the best friend so abrupt that all the armor and walls in the universe are called in to protect the secret!

Remember that you are (hopefully) in the process of recovery from all this. Don't forget how you felt all the months or years that you helped perpetuate your own family secret by protecting it! That's how your friend Kate felt, and if the "walls" are still there for you to feel, then she is still protecting for all she's worth!

To keep treating the imagined stigma, keep referring back to how good it feels to not have to hide things anymore. "Mom's excited about her new women's group on Tuesday nights," you might volunteer. "Things are so different since we all started getting help!"

People go to such great lengths to hide their family secrets when it is not necessary. I'll never forget a wonderful family we treated several years ago at Gateway. Terry was an important executive with a major airline. His wife, Phyliss, taught in a local school district and was in line for a promotion to a principalship, something she had wanted for a long time.

They had a teenage son and daughter who were both very active in the high school and both very popular. Terry had become so dysfunctional because of drinking that his supervisor had lodged a complaint, and through the employee assistance program, the whole family had come into treatment.

They spent the next six months doing some of the best work that any family has ever done in our place. We were all so proud of the way Terry, Phyliss, and the kids had attended their sessions, gone through individual and family therapy, and increased their knowledge of alcoholism by attending our lecture series.

We hold a small but important graduation at the end of the six months, giving everyone who has completed the program an opportunity to share his or her experiences with the people who are currently going through treatment—a way to offer encouragement and share anecdotes of treatment with one another.

At Terry and Phyliss's graduation, my partner, Paul Staley, and I gathered everyone in Paul's office to brief them on what was expected of them for the graduation. As is our custom, we ask them privately what they are most proud of in relation to treatment.

Terry, fairly defiant in his attitude, spoke right up: "You want to know what I'm most proud of?" Everyone quieted down to listen. "I'll tell you what; not a damned soul knows that we're here in treatment!"

It certainly wasn't what Paul or I had expected. This family had worked so hard in treatment, coming back from such a dysfunctional state to a really well-communicating family, that we were both stunned, to say the least, that *this* was the thing of which Terry was so proud.

Paul and.I looked at each other, hoping that Phyliss or maybe one of the Davis teenagers would add something of more substance, but, no, they let their father's statement stand. And then the family secret was burst like a giant fireworks display!

Here's what happened: God's truth! Terry headed for the closed door of Paul's office, and as he opened it, everyone heard, "Well, hi, boss!"

Sure enough, Terry's big boss was standing in the lobby and was attending this graduation as the first event in his *own* enrollment for treatment of alcoholism!

In itself, that could be the story: this family, working so hard to protect its secret and the stigma that Terry felt it carried, "blown" after six months, without any further control on their part.

But the real ending to this little tale happened just recently. One of my daughters and I were waiting in the Red Carpet Room of the airport, awaiting her outbound flight. From across the room, Terry came bounding over, pumped my hand, and— beaming from ear to ear—announced not only for my daughter to hear, but almost *anyone* within fifteen yards, "Hey, Jack! It's been *four years* of sobriety for me! I'm on my way to Washington to celebrate with the family!"

Well, I *finally* had the opportunity to introduce Terry to my daughter, to shake his hand some more, and listen to him fairly regurgitate all that had happened since he gained sobriety and since he and the family had gone through treatment!

Here was a guy who had guarded his family secret with more zeal than anyone we had ever seen, now practically shouting his wellness from the rooftops! The stigma was gone for Terry; he told us of having finally left the airline and opening his own consulting business. Things had changed for him, Phyliss, and the children! He was a very happy camper indeed!

But keeping the family secret is not merely something adults do. Children feel intense peer pressure and the stigma that revealing the secret will surely cause. Adam, eight years old, was a good example of the lengths to which children will go to protect the family secret.

Adam and about eight other youngsters were all sharing their experiences of the previous weekend with their group therapist. At the same time, but in another group, parents were talking with their therapist about the same weekend. Adam's father and mother had had a bitter quarrel, since the father had relapsed in a bar, where he had taken Adam, ostensibly just to watch a football game with some friends. They were not going to stay long, only for a quarter of an hour, and then Adam and his father had planned to go to a movie as part of their weekend together.

But Adam's father, Chet, had decided he could handle a couple of beers, and the movie never happened. Chet's wife, Alice, was, of course, furious. She had wanted to quit treatment, get the divorce she had been talked out of when they entered treatment, and go on with her and Adam's life.

As was the custom, we brought the group of parents and the group of youngsters together toward the end of the Saturday session in what was called then a Family Circle. After everyone was assembled in a big circle, a third therapist, who had not been involved in either of the closed groups of the parents or the youngsters, invited either kids or grown-ups to share an experience of the weekend.

Adam's hand shot skyward.

"OK, Adam," the therapist urged. "What do you want to share with us?"

Adam got to his feet in front of the encircled parents and his peers and proceeded to weave a tale of magic: "My dad took me to the football game!" he blurted out. Before any of us who knew the true story could react, Adam continued his spellbinding story: "And Dad bought me peanuts and popcorn and *plenty* of

Coke!" And then, beaming, he sat down at his place in the circle.

Adam's parents just looked around the room; they said nothing to contradict their son's story! The family secret was going to be kept safe, at least in front of Adam's peers, even though all the other parents knew from hearing it in group that Adam's dad had stayed at the bar and gotten soused.

The peanuts-and-popcorn bit was true enough; Adam kept eating the bar food as well as drinking the bar Cokes set up for him. Of course, his dad's taking Adam to the football game was an outright lie. They had seen the game in the bar on television but were miles away from the stadium. Adam had done what he needed to do; he was preventing the stigma of having the only parent in the group who had relapsed. He had succeeded in protecting this family secret from his peers, and his parents went along with the deception.

All of the therapists were amazed that this had happened so quickly. Adam, in his group, had appeared subdued and somewhat reluctant to share much of anything, while the other youngsters were relating having had pretty good weekends. There was simply *no way* Adam was going to tell his peers how miserable it had been for him! In fact, he chose to fabricate the half-truths to prevent stigma and to protect the latest of the family secrets.

Therefore, I urge you to confront behavior from friends, peers, co-workers, neighbors, whomever, when that behavior seems to be based on the person's knowledge of your family secret. You want to get well, not stay sick, and it is better for you to acknowledge the feeling of discomfort these other people might have with regard to the secret than to let it go unchallenged, thus perpetuating it and building the paranoia for you.

Keep using the tools that you are being given until they are second nature for you. Remember that the other person's discomfort is what you are challenging, *not* your own! If you continue to be positive and open about how well your family is striving to be, you will take the burden of guilt off the friend, neighbor, or co-worker who is struggling with finding a way either not to talk about it with you or not to let you know about his or her own problem.

Finally, remember, there is no stigma to getting well; the stigma is in remaining sick, in having knowledge and ability to make changes that will help your family get well and then doing nothing about it. Don't be guilty of that!

14

Preventive Maintenance

You're infinitely better, and certainly deserving of an "unlimited warranty," much as if you purchased a new car! You are making some changes in your life, and there is no reason to assume that these changes are going to go bad or be defective or need to be replaced.

However, as with most warranties, you must perform some routine but necessary preventive maintenance. It's *so* easy to slip back into the old ways that, before you may even be aware, you are once again becoming a victim of the family secret. So this chapter discusses preventive maintenance by the two principal players: you and the family.

The biggest trap for you may be your willingness to take the responsibility for whatever is going on. Reread Chapter 4, "Fixing the Responsibility," so that you are constantly aware of who the responsible party is in whatever problem is beginning to take place.

As you see the problem develop, treat it as if you are mapping out a major storm front moving into your area. Of course, that's exactly what it is anyway, so you aren't too far afield! You can see the "storm clouds" brewing, and you can almost predict when and where they are going to be at their blackest. Rely on your experience, and then see yourself taking yourself out of the path of that storm. If you are aware that the thing is moving and building rapidly, then you have time to avoid all the hardships and heartaches of a major storm.

It's no different within family circles. If you see a family member start to gather up for a major blowout, ask yourself whether this is going to be laid at your doorstep and, if so, how you will avoid it. If Dad is going to have too much to drink on Christmas Eve and start another family argument, is it because you have done something to upset him? Or is it because Dad has *always* gotten out of hand on Christmas Eve, whether you were around or not?

There are so many instances of young family members who are striking out on their own, trying against some pretty large odds to make their own way in the world. In far too many family circles, some family member starts to brew a major storm over the kid leaving the nest. Everything that goes wrong is because he or she is moving away, and all the storm clouds that have been brewing up *anyway* get lodged and thrown in the face of the young person who is trying to flee the nest.

You may find yourself right in the middle of this storm, playing the switchboard operator and getting so fouled up in the bickering that you wonder what happened! What you are experiencing is a really good case of passive-aggressive behavior. Mom or Dad or your older sister can't handle the fact that your younger brother has decided to move away from the old homestead and try life on his own. You suddenly find yourself the target of all sorts of horse hockey and start screaming (inside and possibly a little on the outside), "What in hell did I do?"

The answer, of course, is that you didn't do anything, but whoever is feeling the most pain can't acknowledge it or communicate directly with the "offending" son who's moving away.

The hurting person just reverts to the sick habits of the past and starts nailing you! Step out of the picture and confront that kind of behavior.

Another family secret says Mom or Dad can't handle the kids not being the parents' full-time entertainment committee. That problem is already taking root and will blossom and grow unless you confront it!

Make sure that you have this example clear in your mind. The family secret isn't the fact that Mom or Dad is showing this passive-aggressive behavior to you; it is the fact that they won't admit that they need their kid(s) for all of their life's needs to be met! *That's* why it's so necessary for you to be able to step back from the brewing storm and ask yourself all the old questions again: "What's going on here?"; "Whose problem is this anyway?"; and "What can I do about it?"

If you have played the role of rescuer in your family, you didn't give the rightful parties the opportunity to work out the problems themselves. Your pain at being in a dysfunctional family has been so great that you were willing to do *anything* to bring peace back into the family. Of course, as you already know, this rationale is based on faulty thinking; the real antagonists and protagonists are never given the opportunity to be aware of the consequences of their sick behavior, because you have stepped in and tried to make things "right."

So be careful and act very slowly when you see the storm clouds descending. Take out your tools of "I feel" statements, so that you are clearly getting the other parties to own the responsibility.

Remember that if guilt has been your constant companion, you want to get rid of it! It will be a lot easier for you to slip back into this guilt than you realize; your general codependency will make that possible. In other words, you take on the sickness and the actions of the really sick person yourself, preferring to handle it with your guilt than with definitive action that causes the truly responsible parties to take a look at themselves.

"Mom and Dad, what makes Tom's leaving so hard on you?" That's a question that could provoke the opening up of the family secret. If it doesn't and you believe that there *is* a secret, you can confront your parents by saying, "I feel that you two are simply afraid that, with Tommy out of the house, you will have to be alone with each other!"

That ought to be enough to extract whatever thorn is sticking in the family's side. This will take a lot of personal courage, but it's very important if you are going to do your own preventive maintenance. If you *don't* ask these kinds of tough questions and make "I feel" statements, you will fall right back into the black hole quicker than Peter Rabbit fell into Mr. McGruder's trap!

Another part of your personal plan of upkeep is for you to periodically check your own position with every other member of your family. Family members rotate positions depending on who is playing what particular role in the family. If you have a sibling who has achieved something and you see the other family members shifting their attitudes toward *you*, then once again, rip off the mask and confront the new behavior. "Hey, wait a minute!" you say. "Just because Elizabeth has been accepted in graduate school doesn't mean that *I* now assume her half of the apartment rent!"

This situation occurred with two sisters, Helen and Lisa, who were sharing the cost of an apartment (with Dad's sly help sometimes). When Helen made it into graduate school, she began to talk about the "added costs" to her, and Lisa, who had a very good job, found herself picking up more and more of the little extras such as the cable TV payments and underground parking for their car, which they also shared.

The family secret was that Dad had been slipping extra bucks to Lisa all along as a way of "making up" for the fact that she wasn't in college and for the way the parents were constantly applauding and planting laurel wreaths on the head of the academically inclined sibling.

When the issue of graduate school became a major "storm

front," Dad didn't want his wife to know that he had been subsidizing Lisa, so he was willing to up the ante to carry on the front that she was doing so well she could take up the slack for her older sister.

Fortunately, Lisa decided to blow the whistle on this particular family secret. She chose a Sunday family dinner to disclose the whole business. You can imagine that there was a stony silence from the wife and mother, who rightly felt betrayed by her husband.

Helen was indignant that she had been "subjected" to this "outrage" (disclosure), and of course Lisa quickly felt herself falling out of the position she had occupied in the family before and sliding right down into the basement! Still, the risk was necessary, and the family began to discuss things as they really were instead of in terms of the fantasy in which Lisa and her father had allowed them all to operate.

After a while and long after the money issue had been settled, Lisa realized she was *still* occupying the cellar position in the family of six.

"I decided," she told me, "to do a little preventive maintenance on myself, the way you had cautioned me to do. I confronted Mom first by asking her what I needed to do to get back in her good graces."

"Of course, she denied that you were in *bad* graces at all, right?" I interjected.

"You've got it! She denied and protested, 'What could I ever be *thinking* of?' and 'Whatever put *that* idea in your head?' But I used a feeling statement and simply told her that ever since the bit about Dad's and my money deal was brought up, I felt that she didn't think much of me."

"How did she react?" I prodded.

"She finally said that maybe I was right and that what bothered her most was that she had felt left out of the plan to help me, and wondered what was wrong that I couldn't confide in her about *my* money situation."

Lisa went on to say that she realized she had been living a family secret of her own by telling her parents, particularly her mother, how well off she was. Helen had, of course, already bought into that, too, so she just naturally didn't think it would be a big deal for Lisa to add a few extra bucks for the apartment rent.

Lisa and her mother worked hard to rebuild trust between themselves. Once that was achieved, Lisa began to sense her position in the family rising from its pit spot to one of more respect. For her, the preventative maintenance stopped a new problem from developing.

When you are doing preventive maintenance for the family, you will need to be as open and confrontational with them as you were with yourself. You will want to say things such as, "Hey, folks, are we starting *another* family secret here?" or, "I feel as if we might be slipping back into the old ways. Anyone else have that same feeling?" Both of these are up-front statements.

If the rest of the family challenges your words, you will need to back up your feelings with facts. Therefore, the tool for you to be using in recovery from the family-secret trap is to maintain a pretty close inventory of how the family is doing. I like to have my patients keep a journal. They all complain about "not having time to write" and being "too tired at night," but I just wave off all these excuses and *insist* that they keep a daily journal.

You should do the same. Here are some tips:

- Write *something* every day! It doesn't have to be long.
- Make sure you write about the *event*.
- Write about how you *felt* over the event.
- Record the participants in the event. Who was involved?
- Record what made you think the family was acting in the "old ways."
- Record the *good* things that happen, too!

These are just some guidelines to spur you on. You can use a yellow pad, a Big Chief tablet, a spiral notebook, or a padlocked, expensive, hand-tooled leather book! What matters is that you *write*. It will help you in sorting your feelings, giving you the opportunity to decide what happened that made you feel the way you did. It also gives you the chance to go back and reexamine the data so that when you confront the family, you will be sure of your ground.

Remember, your journal is just a reference tool for your preventive maintenance, not a book of indictments against every family member.

Probably the most important element of preventive maintenance for you *and* your family is to keep talking to each other! So often, particularly after initial treatment, the family quickly settles back into the old ways of silence. Remember, people do this because it is comfortable; you need to keep spurring folks into open conversation.

Along with the talking, it is of utmost importance that you all continue to attend the support group(s) and the individual counseling that you have been receiving. Although it can be a drag to keep making appointments that take you away, perhaps in the evenings, you *need* this kind of help.

Take a look at how long you and your family have been hurting from the effects of the family secret(s). Won't you at least invest an *equal* amount of time in getting well?

Let's summarize with a checklist of the preventive maintenance you *must* do to avoid slipping back:

1. Keep talking! Don't let "silent battering" get started again.
2. Always make a periodic check of your place in the family.
3. If you have changed positions, determine what has caused it.
4. Keep attending your support groups.
5. Confront behavior as it happens.
6. Take compliments from outsiders about changes they

see, and *pass them on* to the family member(s) involved.
7. Keep fixing responsibility for behavior; put it where it belongs!
8. Keep yourself off the guilt trip; assume blame only when it belongs to you.
9. Watch carefully for another family secret to start to grow, and nip it in the bud! A new secret is your enemy.
10. Write in your journal *daily*. It's your reality check about how things really are going.

This list can be added to, but not deleted from! If you want to add things that more specifically apply to your family situation, feel free to do so. But every one of the ten items is necessary to keep your preventive maintenance going and, therefore, your "warranty" good and in full force!

15
Enjoying the Healing

There just *has* to be a payoff for all the hard work you've been doing, and there *is!* Watching a family get well is one of the most satisfying elements to my being a therapist. You don't have to be in the profession to enjoy healing that involves you and the ones you love.

Furthermore, getting well is fun! A lot of folks have a difficult time with that concept, but in fact you will *enjoy* a family that has begun to break the chains of family secrets.

One of the things that will become apparent to you is that the family suddenly (it seems) *enjoys* being together. You may have taken this for granted, but the minute you begin to see signs of that enjoyment, you will be aware that it *is* something new!

Most families will band together around crises; that is the nature of the herd, to protect each other. But when you see families beginning to come together for the sheer fun of it, then that is a sign of wellness. You can participate in all this; you can monitor the progress and record your findings in your journal. Even more importantly, you can be a part of the process.

So, imagine that you are in the healing process, the stage we call *recovery* from whatever family secret has been particularly devastating to you and your family. It's time for some family fun! How long has it been since you and your family sat down, on the floor or around the dining table, and played a game? Wow! That's pretty radical, isn't it?

Probably you haven't thought about hauling out the old Monopoly set or Trivial Pursuit or one of the popular new games like Pictionary or multiple-tiered Scrabble. The thought of even *suggesting* that the family sit together and not have to talk about the family secret is no doubt a bold one. But go ahead! You have been reading about taking risks throughout this whole book, so this idea isn't unexpected, is it?

It will be up to you to suggest, "Let's turn off the TV and just *try* to play a game together!"

It's scary for other family members to think of letting down the barriers, the defenses, to have *fun*. Those defenses have been up for so long that they will not easily crumble, but you can do it! Just insist and add the real clincher by saying, "I want to see if we can all sit on the floor and play [game] without having to talk about [the family secret]."

This is a bold move on your part because you are flinging wide open the door to your anxiety closet and finding it empty! You are confronting the family with the fact that the only time anyone talks to anyone else is when the person wants to feed the family secret. You are boldly saying, "Maybe we ought to try being a family when there *isn't* a crisis!"

That's exactly what you should do! Be confrontational and carry out your mission. It will be a shock for other family members to hear you say the family secret right out loud, but the shock will quickly wear off, because people will want to quickly bury the thought and go on to what you want to do.

Along with your confrontational behavior, reinforce how great this whole thing can be! "I never thought we could ever have fun again," you say. "Thanks for making it happen."

The others may not know what you're thanking them for, but everyone likes to take credit. So one by one, they will begin to speak up (in a most defensive manner) with, "Whatever made you think we *couldn't* have fun anymore?"

Someone might say, "Oh, Helen, you just get too dramatic! We've *always* enjoyed doing things as a family!" Now *that's* the one remark you were waiting for! Jump on it with a reply that indicates it isn't true at all: "This family hasn't done anything in months except talk about [secret]! But I'm glad that everyone wants to do something now!"

You can put this exchange into your own words. The point is for you to keep nagging until you get a response from someone that allows you to reinforce how the family secret has been holding family interaction down and back.

Working on elaborate jigsaw puzzles is another activity that allows families to start healing together. Buy a new one, bring it home, and just announce, "I'm going to start a new puzzle, and I want everyone to help me!"

There will be some moaning and groaning, and you may hear more griping than you think it's worth, but stand by your guns! Get out a card table, or put the project somewhere where it doesn't have to be picked up every night until it's finished. Encourage everyone to join in putting the puzzle together. You may get only one or maybe *no* takers on your offer, but start anyway.

While you're sitting there working on your puzzle, you can start laying a minor guilt trip on the others who are within earshot. Normally I don't encourage anyone to use guilt as a weapon, but in this case, think of it as a tool to help you get your family motivated. You might say something like this, in the scenario where you have had no takers to work with you on the picture puzzle: "I guess I was wrong," you mutter just loud enough for everyone to hear. "I thought my family could be together and have fun without talking about [family secret]. Guess I misjudged."

That ought to break the logjam! Someone in your family probably can't let a challenging remark like *that* go unanswered.

You'll maybe hear, "What the hell does *that* mean?" and, "Whatever gave you an idea like that? Just because we don't want to do a dumb puzzle," and, "Who appointed *you* the game director, anyhow?"

Well, you can fill in your own family dialogue; these examples give you an idea of what kinds of responses you can expect when you bait the others with a little guilt trip like that. Someone is going to want to jump on your statement and prove you wrong by getting up and joining you in the puzzle project. That's all you wanted in the first place. Of course, if someone persists in wanting to know what your statement means, then you elaborate about how the family secret is all that you have been discussing and that you thought it was time to move on into "wellness things."

You may feel like the family cruise director before all of this is over, but stay with the plan anyhow! The idea is for you and your family to reinvent the wheel. You and your family probably need to relearn how to have fun, and only *you* can push hard enough to make it happen.

I guarantee that your efforts will pay off! You may not get everyone involved in game playing or puzzle building or picnic planning, but you will break through to someone who has been feeling the same way you have felt. The other person just hasn't had the guts to say it, even though in therapy you all should be getting help with interpersonal communications.

Family humor comes into play during these times of enjoying the healing. When was the last time you participated in, say, an April Fool's joke, or when did you go back to the simple little things that make people laugh?

I recall the joy that I saw in a family that went back to celebrating the Twelve Days of Christmas, something they had not done for years. Instead of the big day coming and going, with everyone tearing into their packages, they decided to use Christmas Day as the start of a twelve-day celebration, lasting until the day observing the arrival of the Wise Men with their gifts for the newborn Christ child.

Each day, this family put one little, inexpensive doodad in each other's stockings, to be opened one day at a time. These gifts might include a package of pencils for Dad's workshop, a set of plastic measuring spoons for the family cook, or a set of rubber bands, combs, or bobby pins for others—*little* things that stirred the imagination of the giver and the receiver of the gift also.

To add to the humor and fun of the occasion, all the gifts had been selected by the "Secret Santa" process. The family members had drawn a name of another family member, and then without telling him or her, wrapped each of the twelve little gifts with a clue and simply signed "Your Secret Santa."

The fun came with the reading of the clues by the person opening his or her little stocking gift. The pencil gift was labeled "for someone who is never dull!" Corny? You bet! But it got this family laughing again—or, in this case, *groaning* again at the bad puns!

Another family I was working with reported on an outdoor activity they started. One daughter announced that everyone was going to go ice skating! Well, the hues and cries of protest were heard loud and long on that one, but she prevailed. Everyone went and had a great time, particularly when she kept reinforcing the family healing with comments like, "This is how it *should* be with us!" and, "I'm glad that we haven't forgotten to have *fun* through all this [family secret] business!"

Keep reminding everyone that healing can be *fun*. Often, the owner of a kitchen apron that says, "Are we having fun yet?" may need to be reminded to *read* the apron when someone senses a scowl beginning to be a permanent part of the dinner that he or she is making.

Doing things as a family is not easy; most families with a secret have forgotten how to do it. The presence of the family secret has only added to that difficulty. You will have to take risks with family members. Supposing in the example of the daughter who wanted to go ice skating that someone didn't want to go and was determined to keep everyone else from going. Well, the daughter could put the ball squarely in his or her court by saying, "Then *you* decide what we are going to do today, because this family is going to do *something* together besides sit in front of the TV!"

That may sound pretty bold, particularly if the complainer is a parent, but often when the challenge is hurled in that manner, people *do* respond positively. Always follow up your challenging statements with the reinforcement tool about the family not ever doing things unless the family secret is the main focus.

No one in the family wants to think that he or she has given that much power to the family secret, but that is the case. In the healing process you are all going through, you can confront that over and over.

"My God," you say, "does everyone realize that we haven't done *anything* to celebrate our starting to be a healthy family again?"

That will bring the folks out of their chairs, guaranteed! Why? Because everyone wants to be a winner, and the idea that they might be a part of a losing team just floors them! The losing team, of course, is the family unit that is not celebrating their healing.

There are two kinds of healing. One kind is superficial; let's call it "Band-Aid" healing. It just takes some measures to cover the hurt and provide *temporary* healing. This would be the case in a family that has talked about the secret, brought it out into the open, but just among themselves, and has not sought any long-term treatment to deal with the secret and what it has cost the family.

The second and more complete kind of healing is the "deep wound" kind. Here, you are willing to go beneath the surface and really get to the hurt and cut it out entirely so it can't happen again. This kind of healing requires a commitment to treatment and individual therapy, perhaps over a longer period of time. But the obvious results are more long-term also.

In your healing processes, evaluate the merits of both the Band-Aid and the deep wound healing. Both are necessary in some cases, and you will use both in the healing process of having fun and humor in your life as a family. An example of the Band-Aid approach would be trying a board game or puzzle once and never trying to do anything again. That would have some worth as a temporary measure, but the long-term thrust would be very weak indeed.

An example of the deep wound treatment would be for your family to agree on a family function (such as the ice-skating caper) once a month, with family members rotating on choosing what the special event should be.

Families at our Gateway Treatment Center know how strong we are on this point, and I can't begin to tell you how resistive most of them have been at the beginning of treatment! However, as the plan progresses, the family members begin to take pride in picking out something for the family to do.

One family I worked with had two teenage sons and a teenage daughter. The idea of the whole family agreeing to do anything once a month was about the biggest bomb I had encountered! There was "no way" the kids were going to give up one of their free days or nights to be "stuck" with Mom and Dad, who were recovering from alcoholism.

I brought the entire family together and got them to tell me what they all did for fun in their house. Well, the silence after that question was deafening! This family hadn't done anything except avoid Dad and his drinking and the *secret* of his drinking for so long that they had forgotten about family fun.

The kids stayed away from the house as much as they could; Mom had become like another kid with them, and the battle lines had been drawn tightly! But in recovery, the family could envision change, and that was what we were after. So I proposed that each family member take a turn at selecting what the activity would be for the week. The first grumble was that I was making them agree to a *weekly* family function to start. They had known about the monthly plan, but now I was seeking *more* of their precious private time!

But we prevailed and made the thing even more democratic by having each family member put his or her name into a hat. The "grand drawing" was held in my office during their family therapy session. As luck would have it, one of the boys drew his name first, and with a devilish glee decided that the whole family was going to go to an auto show, an event strictly to the dislike of *everyone* else in the family!

But the rules are solid! Fair's fair, and the family had agreed they would abide with the decision, at least until everyone had a turn. At that point, I had agreed the family could evaluate the results and either abandon the project after the five-week trial run (Band-Aid approach), or go on until at least the end of family treatment (deep wound).

Well, the family, kicking and screaming all the way, went to the auto show, and guess what? They had a *good* time! The son who had "forced" the issue of going was really proud to show his sister a car that he thought would be particularly good for her at college, even though they couldn't afford it. He was patient in explaining to the other family members things that shocked and surprised them; they had neglected his avid interest in cars for so long (Dad's drinking had had the spotlight) that they hardly knew the assured young man who was imparting not only his knowledge of the cars but his ability to talk *to* them and not *down* to them.

Funny thing was, this son thought he was going to "punish" all of them by forcing them to go to the auto show. His sister had recoiled with "Bizarre!" when he announced it. His mother begged him to think of something else; his dad didn't really want to do anything but criticize everyone else, and his brother thought it "would be a real drag" to "waste" their time.

But the more the family members got used to the idea of

doing something together, the more they were all willing to give it a shot. Of course, they always had me to blame for "forcing" this on them, and they were prepared to do just that! However, the evening went well; dad bought everyone hot dogs, popcorn, Cokes, and cotton candy. Mom tried out a couple of the exhibits and actually shared in their group session the following week that she had had "a great time." Surprise!

It went on from there for the five weeks I had gotten them to commit to the project. The other events were a hiking trip that lasted for an overnight (selected by the other son), pizza and a movie (Mom), roller skating and dinner afterward (the daughter), and finally a fishing weekend where Dad actually *helped* everyone else catch some fish! They threw in a baseball game to start the second cycle and were actually planning ahead for the events that were to be their responsibility. The family was starting to have fun!

At the same time that the family was engaging in a weekly event, I was asking the husband and wife to go back to the dating game. I insisted that they spend one night a week without the kids, doing whatever they wanted. Again, the husband and the wife took turns in planning their weekly "date."

We have had Christmas cards, cookies, calls, and personal visits from this family in the months since they left us. They cannot thank the program enough for getting them to go deeper into the healing process. They have modified their family schedules to accommodate college and work demands, but they still do at least two family functions a month, and the couple have made a weekly date a very high priority on their wellness list! Need I say that the husband has remained alcohol-free and that they are a family in the best of recovery?

With these examples in mind, you are ready to pick up the tools we have been exploring and go it alone. You will do well if you have followed the plan to get rid of the family secret as described from the beginning of this book. There is absolutely no reason for you to go on hurting! You are entitled to *healing*.

Furthermore, you are entitled to a life that leaves you breathing free from whatever the family secret that has kept you so bound.

Review the tools that are within these pages. Use them to keep a healthy outlook for yourself and your family, vowing never to slip again back into the furthest reaches of your closet of anxiety.

For you, the path is clear. You can continue to stay sick and, most surely, get even sicker, caught up in the tangled web of one family secret after another, or you can break the cycle of despair, guilt, anxiety, fear, and helplessness.

Getting well is a *family* project. You are the foreman of that project, and this book is at least one set of blueprints that you can follow to the completion of a new, gleaming, and infinitely brighter and stronger family structure than you ever imagined possible!